✓

73

Young, Bob, 1916-1969.
  Liberators of Latin America ₍by₎ Bob and Jan Young.
New York, Lothrop, Lee & Shepard Co. ₍1970₎

  224 p. illus., maps, ports. 22 cm. $4.95

  Concentrates on nine Latin Americans who worked for the freedom of the Spanish dominated colonies.
    Bibliography: p. ₍220₎

  1. Latin America — Biography — Juvenile literature. ₍1. Latin
America—Biography₎ i. Young, Jan, 1919- joint author. II.
Title.

T   F1407.Y6   1970   70-120166
                                 980'.02'0922 [B] [920]
                                                    MARC

Liberators
of Latin America

Liberators
of Latin America
Bob and Jan Young

ILLUSTRATED WITH PHOTOGRAPHS

Lothrop, Lee & Shepard Co.

NEW YORK

Biog Index

Photographs by courtesy of the Organization of American States

Library of Congress Catalog card number: 70-120166

1 2 3 4 5 74 73 72 71 70

ACKNOWLEDGMENT

To the Organization of American States, the Columbus Memorial Library, and Kenneth C. Turner, Photograph Librarian, for their generous assistance in supplying the photographs for this book.

▦ Contents

ATLANTIC OCEAN

Viceroyalty of New Spain

Cuba

Haiti (Saint Domingue)

Puerto Rico

Santo Domingo

PACIFIC OCEAN

Viceroyalty of
New Granada

Guiana

Brazil

Viceroyalty of Peru

Viceroyalty of La Plata

Major political divisions in Latin America before the battles for independence.

1 ⌗ The Long Wait

SETTING THE STAGE

From the founding of the first settlement at Jamestown, Virginia, to the final battle of the Revolutionary War, it took the American colonists one hundred and seventy-five years to gain their independence as the republic of the United States. In the tales of courage and heroism that surrounded our own American Revolution, it is sometimes easy for Americans to forget that the rest of North and South America were also under European control and that the countries of Central and South America had to fight their own separate wars for independence. For the people of these Latin American countries, the wait for freedom was more than three hundred years.

In 1492, on his first voyage of discovery to America, Columbus left 39 men to found the first Spanish settlement on the Caribbean island he called Hispaniola, the island that is jointly occupied today by Haiti and the Dominican Republic. It was not a preplanned settlement; the Santa María had gone aground and there was not enough room on the smaller Pinta and Niña to take all the men home. In 1493, when Columbus returned, he found that these original settlers had perished; however, this time he had brought 1500 men with him. Moving along the coast of the same island into what is now the Dominican Republic, they founded the town of Isabela, the first permanent settlement in the New World.

Once the news of the wealth to be found in America reached Spain more expeditions followed. Settlements spread to the other islands of the Caribbean Sea and to the mainland at the Isthmus of Panama. By 1520 Hernando Cortés had conquered Mexico; less than twenty years later, Francisco Pizarro had seized Peru and sent his armies into Chile and Ecuador. Other expeditions, moving down the east coast of South America, established colonies in Venezuela and Argentina.

At the time of Columbus' discovery, Spain was the leading sea power of the world and one of Europe's wealthiest nations. Less influential as a world power but equal to Spain in the daring of her seafaring explorers, was Spain's smaller neighbor, Portugal. Portuguese vessels had already explored the west coast of Africa. Both nations were Catholic, and in 1493 Pope Alexander VI issued a decree drawing an imaginary line of demarcation from the north to the south poles, 100 leagues west of the Azores and Cape Verde Islands, giving Portugal claim to all discoveries east of that line and Spain claim to all discoveries to the west. When the Portuguese monarchs became dissatisfied with their share, the Treaty of Tordesillas moved the line another 270 leagues west.

While non-Catholic nations might dispute the Pope's right to arbitrarily divide the world, the line was intended to guarantee Portuguese claims in Africa and Spanish claims in the New World and to avert future dispute between the countries. At the time of the decree and treaty, exploration of the South American coast had barely begun. Portuguese explorers followed Columbus in South American waters. When the line of demarcation was finally extended, it was found that the great eastern bulge of South America, which includes Brazil, reached over the line onto the Portuguese side. By 1532 the first Portuguese settlement had been established, making Brazil the single large Portuguese colony in South America.

Then, as today, Brazil occupied almost one-half of the total land mass of South America. Curled around it in the shape of a large letter C, from Argentina and Venezuela on the Atlantic, and running the entire length of the Pacific coast, were the colonies of Spain. In addition, Spain owned all of Mexico and Central America.

The enormous wealth in gold and silver that the Spanish galleons were carrying back to Spain from the New World aroused the jealousy of the other European nations. Following the defeat of the Spanish Armada by England in 1588, Spain began a gradual decline as a sea and world power. During the seventeenth century, French, Dutch, and English pirates and privateers carried on attacks on Spanish ships from hidden bases in the Caribbean Sea. As a result, a number of the islands—such as Haiti (western part of Hispaniola), Curaçao and Jamaica—passed into French, Dutch, or English possession, and the small colonies of British, Dutch, and French Guiana and British Honduras were established on the mainland. But on the whole, Spain kept her great mainland-empire intact. At the time of the Latin American Revolution, the Spanish colonies were not separated into the political divisions we know today. Instead, they were broken into four major political segments called viceroyalties—each ruled by a viceroy—and three smaller political entities called captain-generalcies—each ruled by a captain-general. The four major divisions were the Viceroyalty of New Spain (Mexico), the Viceroyalty of New Granada (Panama, Colombia, Ecuador), the Viceroyalty of Peru (Peru, Bolivia), and the Viceroyalty of La Plata (Argentina, Uruguay, Paraguay). In addition, there were the Captain-Generalcies of Venezuela, Chile, and Guatemala, the latter including the present Central American countries of Guatemala, Nicaragua, Honduras, El Salvador, and Costa Rica. Though granted independent rule, in times of major decision each captain-generalcy was considered a satellite to one of the larger viceroyalties. Thus, Venezuela was subordinate to the Viceroyalty of New Granada, Chile to the Viceroyalty of Peru, and Guatemala to the Viceroyalty of New Spain.

Spanish colonial policy was neither wise nor foresighted. Since Spain was a devoutly Catholic nation, the church was used as an instrument of colonization. Millions of Indians were converted and beautiful cathedrals were erected throughout Latin America, but the lot of the Indians remained poor. Spain did not allow her colonies to trade with other countries or to develop skilled trades or light industry, in the belief that products manufactured in the colonies might compete with those produced by Spanish workers. The Latin American countries developed no large middle class, such as was found in the United States. In Latin America one was either a landowner and very rich, or a worker or slave and very poor.

Spain's major interest in her colonies was in the raw products produced by colonial mines and plantations. At first the Europeans forced the Indians to work in the mines and on coffee, sugar, tobacco, and copra plantations. As the Indians began to die by the thousands, the landowners realized that the natives could not survive the exhausting forced labor. Portuguese Brazil was first to solve this problem by importing Negro slaves from her African possessions. Soon Portuguese ships were bringing more slaves to be sold to the Spaniards. Slave labor began to replace Indian labor, particularly on the jungle plantations.

In most of the Latin American countries class lines were drawn by color as well as wealth. At the top of the social scale were the Creoles, the name given to those of pure Spanish blood who had been born in the colonies. The Creoles were the landowners, and down through the generations many of the Creole families became enormously rich. Next on the social scale were the mestizos, or those of mixed Indian and Spanish blood. Still further down were the great mass of Indians, mulattoes, Negroes, and zambos (the name given to those of mixed Indian-Negro blood).

In spite of their seemingly favored position even the wealthy, landowning Creoles were kept in submission to the crown through the office of the Inquisition. In 1478 the Catholic monarchs Ferdinand and Isabella had established the Spanish Inquisition as an instrument to ferret out converted Jews, Moslems, and Protestants suspected of being secretly disloyal to the Church. Those accused were thrown into prison, where they might be held for months, waiting trial, without knowing either the names of their accusers or the nature of the charges against them. When finally brought to trial before a tribunal made up of high-ranking clerics, accusers were allowed to testify from behind screens. If the victim denied the charges, he was often tortured. If he survived, the tribunal could set him free or order his punishment by execution, long imprisonment, or public flogging. The Inquisition lasted more than three hundred years in Spain, sending thousands of innocent persons to death. By the late sixteenth century it had also spread to the New World.

In the colonies the Inquisition never achieved the savagery that it did in Spain. There were fewer executions, the more usual punishment being imprisonment, fines, and confiscation of property. Only Creoles were subject to the Inquisition, Indians and Negroes excluded on the grounds that they could not help reverting to their pagan ways. The major impact of the Inquisition in the New World was that it stifled the thoughts of the people. The Church decided what books could be read, what ideas could be discussed. Separated geographically by hundreds of miles from both Europe and North America, with rigid controls over trade, imports, and all reading material entering the colonies, even the most intelligent Creoles were ignorant of changes taking place in the rest of the world.

In the eighteenth century a wave of new thought, sometimes called "The Enlightenment," began to sweep Europe and spread to America. Liberal and humanitarian writers— Voltaire, Montesquieu, Diderot, and Rousseau in France, and Thomas Paine in America—began to advance a new political philosophy that men were born equal with the right to question existing authorities and set up governments of their own choice. Growing out of this new thought came three great revolutions that changed the course of world history: the American Revolution, the French Revolution, and finally the Latin American Revolution.

At first the American Revolution, from 1775 to 1781, had only small influence on Latin American thought. Spanish trade restrictions permitted Latin American colonists little contact with North America. It was not until the Latin American Revolution was well under way and the rebel colonies had opened channels of communication with the outside world that the United States became one of the inspirations of their struggle, and many colonies began to pattern their new constitutions after the United States Constitution.

The French Revolution of 1789–1793, overthrowing the French monarchy and establishing a republic in France, initially played a more-important role in influencing Latin American thinking. Many of the wealthy Creole families sent their children to Europe to be educated. There they were influenced by the French writers of that day, learning for the first time of this new political philosophy that avowed that men were born equal and had the right to choose their own political institutions. These were heady ideas for those whose thinking had been rigidly confined since birth. Some of the men who were to lead South America's struggle for independence were in Europe at the time of the French Revolution and were eyewitnesses to its events. However, as much as some of these Creoles might dream of seeing their own countries liberated, they were a minority in their homeland and knew they would have to wait for the right time.

In 1808, due to changing circumstances in Europe, this right time suddenly arrived. Following the French Revolution, the French republican armies found themselves at war with most of the monarchies of Europe. The fighting went poorly for the French until a young Corsican officer named Napoleon Bonaparte began to win victories. Napoleon became the national hero. He was elected first consul of France. By 1804 he had made himself emperor, and his triumphant armies seemed destined to conquer all of Europe.

Spain was ruled by Charles IV, a weak king who idled away his time at his hunting lodges and left the government of the country to others. Early in the struggle, Spain withdrew from the fighting and formed an uneasy alliance with France, hoping by this means to preserve the Spanish throne. In 1807, Charles IV watched nervously as Napoleon's armies invaded Portugal. The Portuguese monarchs and their court embarked for South America, where they set up the seat of their temporarily vanquished government in the colony of Brazil. Because of this allegiance between king and colonists, Brazil was to achieve her independence without the bloodshed that marked the struggle of the Spanish colonies.

Too late, Charles IV realized that Spain was next on Napoleon's invasion list. He abdicated in favor of his son, Ferdinand VII, but Ferdinand VII was forced to abdicate also. Napoleon put his own brother, Joseph Bonaparte, on the throne of Spain. What was left of the Spanish government fled south to Cádiz, where they set up temporary self-rule and joined England in continuing the fight against Napoleon.

Word that Ferdinand VII had been dethroned and replaced by Joseph Bonaparte was the spark that set off the Latin American Revolution. In most of the colonies the wealthy Creoles banded together, rejected the new representatives sent by France, and set up independent *juntas,* or councils, to rule until Ferdinand was returned to the throne. It was not a full-fledged revolution at first. The shock of the French invasion brought a wave of patriotic feeling for deposed King Ferdinand. While setting up institutions of self-government, almost all the South American countries professed loyalty to Ferdinand. But in many of the *juntas* there were liberal Creoles whose real interest was complete independence. As enthusiasm for Ferdinand waned, these liberals gained control, and gradually one colony after another declared complete independence.

By 1814, when Spanish and Portuguese volunteers fighting beside the English army had brought about the defeat of Napoleon and restored Ferdinand to the throne, most of the colonies had already declared their independence. Spanish troops, newly released from fighting Napoleon, were shipped to South America to put down the rebellions. The following years were the darkest for the revolutionary cause, as one small republic after another fell before the powerful Spanish army. However, the remnants of the revolutionary forces united under two great leaders. San Martín of Argentina and Bolívar of Venezuela refused to give up. From remote hideaways in the interior, they reorganized their forces for a final assault on the enemy. Country after country was retaken, and at the Battle of Ayacucho, in 1824, the last of the Spanish generals was forced to surrender.

Though North and South America shared a goal of liberation from the mother country, there were many differences between the Latin American Revolution and our American Revolution. In Latin America, the rebellion was not a popular cause at first but mainly the vision of a handful of Creole landowners. The mass of people, illiterate, poverty-striken, and apathetic, cared little whether they were free or subjects of Spain.

Often Latin American leaders quarreled among themselves, and civil wars over the kind of government to be established were waged side by side with the war against the Spanish forces. Slavery, which was not an issue in the United States until years later, was an important issue in the Latin American revolutions. Haiti, the first successful Latin American republic, gained her freedom through a revolt of the slaves. In other South American countries the abolishment of slavery was written into the first constitutions. Freed slaves fought beside their former masters against the Spaniards. In Mexico, the revolution also became a war of social reform, with the wealthy landowners pitted against the lower classes.

The American Revolution lasted six years, the Latin American Revolution nearly twenty. Just as the American Revolution produced George Washington, Nathan Hale, George Rogers Clark, Marquis de Lafayette, and other heroes, so did the Latin American struggle produce its heroes. It would be impossible to tell all of their stories in a single book. In every country there were men who fought bravely, too often went to martyrs' deaths, and are today honored by their fellow countrymen. That this book has chosen only nine liberators who seemed most representative of the struggle does not lessen either the heroism or contribution of the many other national heroes who have been omitted because of limited space.

2 ▨ Up from Slavery

TOUSSAINT L'OUVERTURE, 1743–1803

By strange coincidence the Caribbean island where Columbus founded the first settlement of the New World was also the scene of the first successful Latin American revolution. Columbus called the island Hispaniola, but the natives called it Haiti. Later, the Spaniards changed the name to Santo Domingo. By the start of the eighteenth century, Spain had lost the western portion of the island to France so that it was divided into the eastern Spanish colony of Santo Domingo (today's Dominican Republic) and the western French colony of Saint Domingue (Haiti). It was in the French section, Haiti, that the first Latin American revolution began as a direct result of the French Revolution, led by a Negro and former slave. Toussaint L'Ouverture, meaning Toussaint "The Opener," was the name he gave himself. His real name was François Dominique Toussaint, and he was born to slave parents sometime around 1743 on the huge Bréda plantation in what is now northern Haiti.

At that time most of the huge island, rising from tropical lowlands along the coast to 6,000-foot mountains in the interior, was divided into plantations with sugar cane as the principal crop. The island's original Indian population had almost disappeared due to white men's diseases and exhausting forced labor. Thousands of Negro slaves had been brought from Africa to replace them, so that the island's population consisted of about 500,000 black or mulatto slaves compared to only 70,000 free men. The latter were divided into the

Creole, white landowners called the "Great Whites," the mulatto landowners called "Little Whites," and a lesser body of mulatto and Negro free men.

In probably no other colony of the New World was the population so race conscious and segregated along color lines. The Creoles, or Great Whites, had been unable to keep the mulattoes, or Little Whites, from gaining ownership of land, usually by inheritance from the mixed marriages of their ancestors. But by law anyone with a trace of Negro blood was excluded from public office. It was a caste system so rigid that a mulatto slave considered himself socially superior to a free black man.

Haiti occupied a world position out of all proportion to its importance today. It provided half of Europe's cotton, coffee, and sugar. The output of its plantations made it France's richest colony and one of the wealthiest countries of the New World. Its two major cities, Cap Français in the north and Port-au-Prince, the capital, compared favorably with New York and major cities of the United States. Cap Français, in particular, was the island's pride with a population of 20,000, paved streets, public squares, fine buildings made of stone with ornate iron-grillwork balconies, open-air markets, and stores offering luxuries from all over the world.

Many of the wealthier landowners chose to live in France, leaving the management of their plantations to overseers, while those who remained on the island lived in splendor equal to that of European nobility. Their furniture, clothing, and dishes were imported from Europe. Since a Creole's importance was judged by the number of his slaves, it was the custom at dinner to have a slave in livery standing behind the chair of each household member and guest.

Contrasting the wealth of the landowners was the abject

poverty of the slaves. They were divided into two classes, household and field slaves. Household slaves, who were usually blacks born on the island, received kinder treatment than the others. They suffered fewer beatings, were sometimes educated by their masters, and occasionally might even be given their freedom as a reward for some special service. The majority of the free Negro population was made up of former household slaves.

The treatment and living conditions of the field slaves were usually worse than those of the landowners' cattle or horses. They worked from sixteen to eighteen hours a day, even longer in harvest season. Flogging was administered for the slightest infraction. For more serious offenses grisly tortures— such as searing with boiling sugar; cutting off ears, tongues, or noses; and burying or burning alive—were common. Slaves awoke in the morning to the crack of the whip and went to bed at night to the moans of their beaten companions. Their birthrate was high but their death rate was even higher, so that a stream of newly seized slaves from Africa poured into the island constantly to replenish the diminishing work force.

Though law decreed that an owner was responsible for supplying his slaves with food and clothing, the statutes were largely ignored. Raising table crops interfered with the landowners' more valuable cultivation of sugar, cotton, and coffee for export. It was the custom to give each slave family a tiny plot of the least-productive ground, where they raised their own food. They bought their clothing with what surplus they could spare for barter in town. Saturdays and Sundays were given them for this extra work.

The law also required that all slaves be baptized in the Catholic faith. They were usually baptized en masse immediately on their arrival. The still-chained slaves were forced to kneel under the overseer's whips while they were hastily baptized, given names, then branded with the marks of their owners. After that few French owners gave any more attention to the slaves' Christian instruction, fearing that the teachings of Christianity would encourage the slaves to rebellion and give them the mistaken belief that they were entitled to be treated like human beings. Many were allowed to pursue their own tribal religions, usually called voodoo, as long as it did not interfere with the owners' work or interests.

Toussaint belonged to the more fortunate class of household slaves. His mother was a cook. The Bréda plantation, located in northern Haiti in the hills overlooking Cap Français, was one of the largest in the colony, with more than a thousand slaves. The owner, a French nobleman, lived abroad, but the Creole manager who ran the plantation was kind, and the Bréda slaves were better treated than those of the majority of the other plantations.

Records were poorly kept in those days, and historians still differ as to who was Toussaint's father. Toussaint's son claimed that he was a famous Arada chieftain and medicine man who, though newly arrived from Africa, had won the favor of the Bréda overseer. He also claimed that another slave, Pierre Baptiste, who worked in a nearby Jesuit hospital, was only Toussaint's godfather. However, all his life Toussaint treated Pierre Baptiste with such love and devotion that a few authorities believe he was actually Toussaint's father. Whatever his paternal background, Toussaint's greatest asset was his intelligence. He spoke the Arada language and learned the secrets of herb medicine, which won him great favor with the field slaves. From Pierre Baptiste he learned to speak, read, and write French, and also learned the teachings of Catholicism, which made him a favorite with his masters.

Shortly before Toussaint's birth, a famed prophetess predicted that the child would be a male and great chief. However, Toussaint was such a frail, sickly baby that at first he was not expected to live. Later, as a spindly youth, he was given the nickname "The Stick" by the other children. Determined to overcome his physical handicaps, Toussaint spent hours exercising and toughening his body. He became so expert at handling horses that years later he was considered one of the finest horsemen on the island. Though his program built up his strength and endurance, all of his life he continued to have a frail appearance. He was only 5 feet, 2 inches tall, with slender limbs, narrow shoulders, and a thin, sunken chest. But he had an appealing, triangular face with a high forehead, large, closely set eyes, small pursed mouth, and very white, pointed teeth.

Like most slave children, he spent his early boyhood helping herd the livestock, but his precocity combined with his skill with animals brought him to the attention of the Creole manager, who eventually advanced him to the coveted position of coachman.

As a result of his favored position and education, Toussaint considered himself superior to the other slaves; but when he was fifteen an event occurred that brought home to him the brotherhood of all the slaves of Haiti. With a friend, Georges Biassou, who worked at the Jesuit Hospital, he had gone for a holiday to the town of Cap Français. Though they had no money to spend, it was a great adventure for the two young boys just to walk the crowded streets, staring at the colorfully dressed crowds and admiring the enticing items offered in the markets. However, this day they were attracted to a huge crowd that had gathered in one of the squares.

Haiti's slaves had found only two methods of protesting mistreatment. On some plantations large numbers of slaves committed mass suicide, by this pitiful means not only releasing themselves from misery but supposedly hurting their masters by depleting work forces and causing a loss of prestige. A second, more direct, method was by poison. Arsenic was used in large quantities on the plantations to combat insect pests, making it easy for a household slave to slip arsenic in his master's food. The more brutal landowners lived in such fear of poisoning that they had their food tested before they ate it.

If a slave succeeded in the poisoning, he usually fled to join other fugitives in the mountains. One of these refugees, named Macandal, was accused of going even further and plotting to distribute packets of poison to destroy the entire French populace of Cap Français. Caught by the authorities, he had been condemned to die by being burned at the stake.

When skinny, little Toussaint and Biassou elbowed and wiggled through the crowd to the center of the square, they found that they had arrived at the moment of Macandal's execution. Toussaint watched in fascinated horror as the torch was applied. Suddenly, with superhuman effort, Macandal burst his chains and plunged toward the crowd, festoons of burned flesh hanging from his seared body. He swept so close that Toussaint could smell the terrible odor of burning flesh. Soldiers charged into the crowd, knocking people indiscriminately to the ground. Recapturing the unfortunate Macandal, they tossed him callously back on the fire, where the flames put an end to his agonized screams.

To Toussaint, who had never even been whipped by his master, the sight had been electrifying. For years he had heard other slaves whisper of the tortures and punishments that took place on some plantations. He had heard of slaves being torn apart by savage dogs, crushed by being bound on wheels, tossed alive into boiling vats of sugar, driven insane by having hot wax poured into their ears. Such cruelty seemed so remote from his life at Bréda that he had not believed the stories. Now he had seen that such things were really happening.

Back at the plantation, Toussaint remained outwardly obedient and diligent, but he had always been a melancholy, brooding youth and he did not forget what he had seen. Even if he wished to improve the lives of his people, he had no means of doing anything. He knew that suicide was no solution, and there would be no point in poisoning the manager at Bréda, who was a kindly master and whom he liked and respected. Toussaint had enough education to believe that any lasting changes would have to come from the French government. He had great faith in the French king, telling himself and others that someday, when the king realized the true misery of the slaves, he would change the laws.

Over the following years Toussaint continued to work hard at Bréda and rose steadily in the favor of the plantation manager. He became manager of the sugar mill and then plantation steward in charge of livestock, a position never before filled by a slave. In this high position he assumed the leadership of Bréda's 1,000 slaves.

In spite of his somewhat unprepossessing appearance, Toussaint was considered quite a ladies' man in his youth and he had numerous sweethearts among the plantation women. But when he was in his mid-thirties he followed the advice of his master and agreed to take a wife. His position was already important enough so that he was not forced to marry the young Arada girl the manager had selected for him. He was allowed to take the wife of his choice, an older woman named Suzanne, who had already borne one son by her former mulatto master. It was a happy marriage. Suzanne bore Toussaint two sons, but he treated all three boys the same.

At the outbreak of the French Revolution, in 1789, Toussaint was forty-five years of age, secure in his position as livestock steward, and seemingly set in his ways. He was old enough by the standards of that time so that he was called "Papa Toussaint" or even "old Toussaint" by his fellow slaves.

The French Revolution brought immediate repercussions in the colony. The Creoles, or Great Whites, viewed it with mixed feelings. They resented the haughty manners of the French officials sent to govern them as well as the high taxes imposed by the government. They welcomed the possibility of being rid of both, but they were less enchanted with the slogan of "Liberty, Equality and Fraternity" shouted by the street mobs of France. They had no intention of giving mulatto landowners a voice in the government. To the mulattoes, or Little Whites, the revolution promised everything: relief from taxes and equality with the Creoles. As the bickering between the two sides increased, fighting erupted. Mulatto landowners, whose greatest strength was concentrated in the south, armed many of their slaves. At first the government representatives, most of whom had been appointed by the monarchy, sided with the Creoles. When an edict granting mulattoes equal citizenship came from France, they arbitrarily suspended it. As months passed and they saw that the French monarchy was doomed, they reversed their stand and urged reconciliation between the Great Whites and the Little Whites. Soon even more alarming rumors reached the islands: the new republican government of France was planning to free the Negroes also. Neither the mulatto nor Creole owners wanted to lose their slaves. United by this new threat, they agreed to a truce, but it was too late to check the revolutionary fervor that had been ignited.

In the two years of bickering and intermittent fighting, the welfare of the island's half-million slaves had been ignored. In the south the mulatto landowners had armed their slaves to fight beside them. These slaves now posed a threat. One entire Negro company that had fought valiantly beside the mulattoes was loaded on a ship, presumably to be transferred to a new location. Once at sea, they were clubbed and thrown overboard to drown.

Even in the Creole-dominated north, the slaves could not be kept ignorant of what was going on in Europe. For centuries a kind of grapevine had spread events of every Creole household to the other plantations. The liveried servants standing behind their masters' chairs carried the conversations of Creoles and their official guests back to the kitchen slaves. The kitchen slaves spread the information to the field hands. It was the custom of slaves from various plantations to meet at night for secret voodoo rites in the forest. There, news was passed on to slaves of other plantations. It was not long before they heard rumors from France that the slaves were to be freed.

A Catholic, Toussaint disapproved of voodoo, but he attended some of the meetings to observe and to exchange ideas. The rumor that they were to be given their freedom was intoxicating to slaves so long held in misery. Though he had long dreamed of freedom for his people, Toussaint still believed it could be achieved by orderly methods of government. A Jamaican Negro from another plantation, named Boukmann, urged the Negroes to take immediate action of their own.

The revolt began on the night of August 22, 1791, when Boukmann led the slaves off his own plantation. As they streamed from their houses, the men armed with knives, axes, and machetes and the women and children carrying their meager household goods, the owners tried to stop them. Seeing they could not, they barricaded themselves in their houses. The slaves made no effort to harm them. They streamed down the road to the next plantation, where more slaves joined them. At first the exodus was orderly, the plan being for the slaves to march to Cap Français, where, they had heard, a contingent of soldiers representing the new French government was about to arrive. There they expected to receive their freedom. As their numbers increased so did the excitement of the marchers. At the Noué plantation violence erupted. The slaves there had old grievances against their masters. They murdered the owner and overseer, ransacked the house, then set it and the cane fields afire. As the flames mounted the crowd went wild. More slaves poured in from other plantations and Boukmann lost control. Slaves harboring hatreds of long standing turned on their masters, torturing and killing them in the grisly manner with which they had once been tortured, then setting fire to everything in sight.

Soon the smoke of the burning cane, coffee, and indigo plantations could be seen for miles as it swept toward Cap Français. The rebel slaves began destroying everything and everyone in their path. In panic, Creoles who had been warned of the advance poured into the city for refuge. On the plantation of Bréda, Toussaint held the slaves in check. Though his sympathies were with the cause of the rabble hordes of Boukmann, years and wisdom made him cautious. He was right. The French soldiers did not welcome the slaves but turned on them, killing hundreds, including Boukmann, whose severed head was displayed on a pole at the city gate. But the revolution could not be halted. To escape the retaliation of the French, hundreds of slaves and free Negroes streamed from the city to join the rebels. Two new leaders, Jean-François and Georges Biassou, rose to take Boukmann's place.

Biassou was the friend who had been with Toussaint on the day he had witnessed the fiery execution of Macandal. He sent repeated notes to Toussaint, urging him to join them. Toussaint waited a month to make up his mind. It was a time of tormenting doubts, for he still had a lingering faith in the power of the government to restore law and order. As the fighting and massacre of his people continued, his faith in the new French government weakened. When he finally made up his mind to join his people, it was a decision from which he never again wavered. A month after the outbreak of the rebellion, he assisted the plantation manager and his family to escape to safety and sent his own family into exile in Spanish-owned Santo Domingo. He ordered the Bréda plantation put to the torch and led Bréda's 1,000 slaves to the rebel camp outside Cap Français.

Because of his delay in joining the rebellion, Toussaint was regarded with suspicion by the other leaders, including Biassou. In spite of the reinforcements he had brought, he was not at first given a military command, but was assigned to the position of "Physician to the Armies" because of his ability as a medicine man. Toussaint accepted the relatively minor post, but soon he was asked more and more often to take part in the discussions at the council table. There he was often annoyed by the ignorance of the other two leaders as well as the way they outfitted themselves in cast-off finery stripped from the whites and strutted about, giving themselves fantastic titles, but he concealed his feelings.

The first two months of the revolution had resulted in the slaughter of nearly 2,000 whites and 10,000 Negroes, and the complete devastation of once-rich territory. While Cap Français could receive supplies by sea, the rebel army suffered terribly from hunger, for in their frenzied burning of the fields they had destroyed their own source of food.

Toussaint silently disagreed with many of the policies of the leaders. Though the Negroes were seemingly unlimited in numbers, he was sickened by the knowledge that thousands of lives had been lost by throwing the primitive, poorly armed blacks in direct frontal attacks on the enemy. He began to drill the men in guerrilla tactics. He taught his men to lie in wait for small groups of French soldiers in the forest, to fall on the soldiers after completely surrounding them, and then to arm themselves with guns taken from the victims. Even so, in the excitement of battle many of the former slaves would suddenly throw away their captured guns, preferring to fight with their more-familiar machetes and knives. In attempts to silence enemy cannon they naïvely thrust their arms down the muzzles, often being blown apart. If lucky enough to capture the cannon, many were so ignorant of sophisticated weapons that they tried to fire the guns by lighting the wrong end.

Seeing that it was impossible to train the great mass of the army, Toussaint concentrated on forming an efficient band of 600 men whom he could trust completely. With these troops he was soon overpowering many of the smaller outposts around Cap Français, though the top command remained in the hands of Jean-François and Biassou.

By this time news of the rebellion had reached Europe. In

September, 1792, three civil commissioners were sent from France along with 6,000 French troops to bring peace to the colony. For a brief period the troops were successful. Toussaint lost almost half of his forces in a single battle; but a few days later, when he led his reorganized men against another French outpost many miles away, the French general, Laveaux, is reported to have said with begrudging admiration, "That Toussaint, he makes an opening everywhere!" When Toussaint heard this he was flattered. Not long afterwards he started signing his name Toussaint L'Ouverture.

The initial successes of the French were short-lived. When Negro and mulatto soldiers finally overran Cap Français, burning most of the town to the ground, thousands of white settlers boarded ships to sail into exile. Many of the Creoles landed in Cuba and Puerto Rico, where their tales of the devastation caused by the rebellion may have played a part in the future of those islands. Later, when the Spanish colonies on the mainland launched their revolutions for independence, Puerto Rico and Cuba remained loyal to Spain. A lesser number of refugees found new homes in the United States. Although their influence was not as strong, they no doubt bolstered the conviction of many southern slave owners that their own slaves should never be freed.

In southern Haiti, other Creoles fled across the border into Spanish Santo Domingo. In 1793, when King Louis XVI was beheaded, Spain and England declared war on France. In Haiti the French army suddenly found itself deserted by its Creole supporters and facing a new war with Spanish forces in Santo Domingo, in addition to the rebellion of the slaves.

Where the French generals considered the slave army and its officers as inferiors, the smaller Spanish forces in Santo Domingo lured them with offers of guns, ammunition, and equal status with their soldiers. With Jean-François and Biassou, Toussaint went over to the side of the Spaniards, professing that he wished to fight for a country that still had a king. However, Toussaint was important enough now to make his own arrangements with the Spaniards, accepting the rank of colonel and taking with him his 600 crack troops. Soon hundreds more slaves crossed the border to join him.

On August 29, 1793, in a desperate attempt to raise an army to fight the Spaniards in the east as well as the British, who were attacking the coastal ports, the French commissioner in Haiti passed a decree freeing the slaves. Toussaint was not impressed, having little faith that the decree would be approved in France.

Toussaint issued his own appeal to the slaves from his camp in Santo Domingo:

> *Brothers and friends. I am Toussaint L'Ouverture, my name is perhaps known to you. I have undertaken vengeance. I want Liberty and Equality to reign in San Domingo. I work to bring them into existence. Unite yourselves to us brothers and fight for the same cause. . . .*
> *Toussaint L'Ouverture*

For a man supposedly fighting for the Spanish king it was a strange statement, but it brought more followers to Toussaint's camp, and as long as he won victories, the Spanish generals were contented. This interval of fighting on the side of the Spaniards brought Toussaint one happiness in his reunion with Suzanne and his children, whom he had sent to refuge in Santo Domingo. Suzanne was bewildered by the changes. She found it hard to believe that her graying ex-slave husband could have become a man of such importance.

During his brief vacation with his family, Toussaint lived simply, going to Mass with Suzanne each day and impressing the Spaniards with his devoutness as a Catholic. But the events taking place were beginning to disturb him. Toussaint was not the only one winning victories. Spain's British allies were landing troops along the coast of Haiti, driving the French forces ahead of them. Toussaint had been unable to get a commitment from the Spaniards to free their slaves, and in all the towns their British allies were capturing, slavery was immediately being restored. Toussaint was becoming more and more disenchanted with his new friends.

In May, 1794, news finally reached the islands that the government of France had ratified the decree of the commissioners. All of Haiti's slaves had been declared free men. This was the goal for which Toussaint had been working: emancipation backed by law. With this news his loyalty to Spain ended. He immediately sent a letter to his former enemy, General Laveaux, offering to return his allegiance to France now that his people had been freed. The communication was supposedly secret, but some of the Spanish officers and Toussaint's old friends Jean-François and Biassou were becoming suspicious of his shifting loyalties. First, some of the soldiers under Toussaint were removed from his command. Next, Jean-François ordered the arrest of several of his officers. Undaunted, Toussaint rode into Jean-François's camp with his brother to demand their release. They were met by gunfire. Toussaint's brother fell dead from his saddle, but Toussaint managed to twirl his mount about and escape to his own headquarters.

Toussaint realized he could no longer wait for an answer

from Laveaux. Hurriedly organizing his loyal followers, he attacked and defeated a group of Spanish soldiers, swept on into Biassou's camp, scattering his forces, then galloped to freedom across the border. Within a few days a reply came from General Laveaux, welcoming Toussaint back to French soil and making him a brigadier general.

It was now necessary for Toussaint to recapture dozens of towns and outposts that only the year before he had seized for the Spaniards, but more than 5,000 soldiers slipped away from the Spanish camps to join him. In addition, he now had the services of two brilliant young officers, Jean Jacques Dessalines and Henri Christophe, both of whom would later play important roles in Haiti's history.

During those next months Toussaint took part in more than two hundred engagements. Though he was over fifty, gray-haired, and still frail in appearance, he possessed astounding endurance. In the field he insisted on eating the same food as his men and sleeping in the open beside them. He had been wounded in battle more than twenty times. Once his hand was crushed while he was trying to help a group of struggling soldiers move a cannon. Another time, he was struck in the face by a spent cannon ball, losing two of his front teeth. Yet for all this display of camaraderie, he retained a certain aloofness and dignity, letting his men know that while he shared their sufferings he still was indisputably their leader.

In Europe, vacillating Charles IV of Spain was beginning to realize he had made a poor decision in opposing France. In 1795 he signed the Treaty of Basle, ending the fighting between their countries. With peace restored between the French and the Spanish, the British were the only foreign power remaining to be driven from Haiti. There was still an

TOUSSAINT L'OUVERTURE

enemy within. The burning and sack of Cap Français had ended the dominance of the Great Whites, but the mulattoes, or Little Whites, were determined to keep the blacks from gaining political power. After a mulatto coup General Laveaux was arrested and thrown into prison at Cap Français. Toussaint then ordered his forces north to free him. By this time Toussaint was the idol of the entire Negro populace. As he rode north so many former slaves rushed to join him that he did not have to fight for Cap Français. He rode into the city unopposed to free the French general.

Politically it was the most astute move Toussaint had ever made. A short time later, when General Laveaux was named governor-general of Haiti, he made Toussaint his lieutenant-governor and announced publicly that he would not do any· thing without consulting Toussaint first.

Toussaint had become the most powerful man in Haiti. Because of his support of the French forces he had also become a hero in Europe, and his sons were sent to France to be educated. Haiti was still far from a peaceful island. The British held Port-au-Prince, the capital, and many of the coastal cities, while the still-militant mulattoes retained a foothold in the far south. After five years of fighting, Toussaint had only one goal: complete freedom for people of Haiti, black or white. Along with the arts of warfare, he had also learned to play politics. Haiti was about to elect two representatives to the French assembly in Paris. By cleverly manipulating the electors, Toussaint saw to it that General Laveaux and the principal French commissioner were elected to the seats. Neither man could gracefully refuse the office and when they set sail for France, Toussaint had rid Haiti of the last two white men of influence.

Toussaint was learning to deal with Europeans. Though inwardly committed to complete independence for his people, he was not ready to reveal these plans to the French. He had found that the best way to please European governments was to win victories. To placate France he turned his attention to driving out the British. He presented the face of a French patriot, but his orders to his battle-scarred troops on the eve of the attack on Port-au-Prince left little doubt that they were fighting for themselves: "Do not disappoint me. Prove yourselves men who know how to value liberty and how to defend it. . . . It is not for booty we are fighting. It will be time enough to think of material things when we have driven the enemy from our shores. We are fighting that liberty—the most precious of all earthly possessions—may not perish."

It was the tendency of white historians and military commanders in those days to blame their losses in the New World on the fevers of the tropics. Yellow fever did kill many European soldiers; but both the French and British had underestimated the ferocity of the Negroes as fighters. On April 14, 1798, when Toussaint made his triumphal entry into Port-au-Prince, a driving rainstorm did not prevent the entire population from turning out to greet him. Toussaint wore a general's uniform but bound around his head was a yellow bandana, which he traditionally wore into battle.

Unlike his generals, Dessalines and Christophe, and many of the earlier Negro leaders, Toussaint had never attempted retaliation against the whites. He did not believe his people had been forced into slavery because of the color of their skin, but because they were weak. He had seen that in spite of their own Negro blood, many mulatto slave owners treated their slaves even more cruelly than the whites. Until the black people produced their own educated class, he believed they would need the help of all the whites who were friendly toward them and who supported their cause.

Shortly after taking Port-au-Prince, he entered into volumi-
nous correspondence with the British commanders who had
withdrawn their forces to the next port to the north. He
offered amnesty for prisoners and generous terms of surrender
if they would leave the island. His policy was rewarded. On
October 5, 1798, Toussaint led his soldiers unopposed into
Môle St. Nicholas as the last of the British troops sailed out
of the harbor.

The ouster of the British brought new accolades for Toussaint from the common people of France; but the French
statesmen were not fools. Already many in the government
were losing their enthusiasm for the "Black Napoleon" who
professed loyalty to France but acted like a liberator.

France was not the only country watching Toussaint with
mounting concern. In the United States southern plantation
owners had listened with indignation to the stories of refugee
Creoles. The American consul to Haiti wrote the secretary of
state, warning that the United States should carefully guard
her neutrality in Great Britain's war with Napoleon, for with
the aid of the French fleet Toussaint's army could easily be
transported to United States soil. Though this was unlikely,
it was not a completely foolish fear. Toussaint's fame as a
general was world-wide. He commanded an army of 50,000,
more than double the number Washington had commanded
during the American Revolution. If a landing was made in
the South, Toussaint would undoubtedly try to get the slaves
of the southern plantations to swell his forces.

Toussaint had no interest in attacking the United States or
adding to Napoleon's glory. Even with British soldiers off
Haitian soil, the British blockade closed most of the island's
ports. Toussaint knew that someday, when the fighting was
over, Haiti would have to rebuild. The starvation that had
followed the burning of plantations around Cap Français in

the first year of the revolution had taught him a grim lesson. Whenever his slave army secured an area, he directed some of the soldiers back to the land to start planting again. He also realized that an island empire could not survive without trade. On July 13, 1799, he signed a treaty with England allowing free trade with Haiti's ports. To make the treaty more acceptable to the French, who were at war with England, he included free trade with the United States in the agreement, though no American signatures appeared on the document.

The French government was not deceived. Before the departure of the British, the French general, the Marquis Theodore Hédouville, had been sent to Haiti, supposedly to help pacify the island but also to keep Toussaint in check. Like other Europeans before him, Hédouville underestimated Toussaint's intelligence and cunning. Believing he was dealing with a primitive black man, he had one of his aides flatter Toussaint in an effort to persuade him to sail to Europe in expectation of great honors. "How flattered I should be . . . if I could take back Toussaint L'Ouverture, who would find in France recognition of his services, honors and a well earned rest," the aide cajoled.

Toussaint was not taken in. "Your vessel is not big enough for a man like me," he replied. When the aide persisted in his arguments Toussaint pointed to a frail, newly planted sapling. "I'll go when this has grown big enough to build my ship."

Finally, in desperation, Hédouville encouraged the hard feelings between the mulattoes and the Negroes in an attempt to break Toussaint's strength. It was a game two could play. Toussaint let the rumor spread that Hédouville had really come to Haiti with the intention of restoring slavery. As thousands of frenzied natives poured into Cap Français from the surrounding plantations, Hédouville was forced to take to his ships and escape to France.

From a skillful military commander, Toussaint was making the transition to a clever politician. The following day he announced to the people that he was tired of fighting and wished to retire to the country estates he had acquired as rewards for his service to Haiti.

The crowds went wild, streaming through the streets crying, "Don't leave us, Papa Toussaint! Don't leave us!" After this demonstration that the people were solidly behind him, Toussaint agreed to remain their leader.

The western coastline of Haiti roughly resembles one side of a huge hourglass. While the British held Port-au-Prince at the nipped-in waistline of the hourglass, it had been impossible for Toussaint to get past them to reach mulatto rebels in the south. Now, with Hédouville on his way home, Toussaint turned to pacifying the south.

The ensuing battles between blacks and mulattoes were among the most bloody the world had ever seen. Soldiers were chopped apart with axes, knives, and cleavers. Atrocities were common as thousands of captives, including women and children, were tortured and slaughtered. Even Toussaint was appalled by the massacre of mulattoes by Dessalines, whom he had placed in charge of the final stages of the campaign. "I told him to prune the tree, not uproot it!" he cried.

Napoleon had a somewhat different comment for the mulatto commander André Rigaud, when he finally escaped the island in defeat and arrived in France with a long list of accusations against Toussaint. "General, I have but one fault to find with you—you have lost," Napoleon said coldly.

With the mulattoes put down, Toussaint continued across the border into Spanish Santo Domingo. According to the Treaty of Basle, Spain had already relinquished Santo Domingo to France with the provision that Spanish troops would remain in control until French troops arrived to replace them. The Spanish soldiers had little inclination to fight for a country their king had given away by treaty five years before. On January 21, 1801, Toussaint rode victoriously into Santo Domingo City, the capital. Following the example of Napoleon, he put aside his general's uniform with its gold braid and medals and entered the city wearing a simple blue uniform and riding a mule.

With the island united, it was no surprise to the world when Toussaint announced on July 7, 1801, that a constitution had been written by an elected assembly of nine men, who had named him governor of Haiti for life. The surprise was at the ability Toussaint showed as a statesman. He had already demonstrated his interest in restoring Haiti's agriculture. Former slaves were sent back to work on the plantations, but with strict laws requiring every man to do his share. Heavy taxes were levied on the plantations to provide the government with a solid economic base. Whites were encouraged to return to their plantations as well as to take administrative posts in the government. Always a devout Catholic, Toussaint passed laws attempting to outlaw the voodoo practices brought from Africa. Most historians agree that if Toussaint had been allowed to follow the path set by the new constitution, Haiti might have flourished as an independent republic.

Unfortunately, Napoleon, who had become first consul of France, could not afford such an affront to French pride. He ordered an expeditionary force to Haiti. Chosen as its leader was the youthful General Charles Leclerc, Napoleon's brother-in-law, husband of his favorite sister, Pauline. The expeditionary force was the largest that France or any other nation had ever assembled until that time. Before the close of 1801, the first contingent of 20,000 troops had left France. By February, 1802, Leclerc with the main body of soldiers was ready to land at Cap Français, while other units were sent along the coast to seize Port-au-Prince and Santo Domingo City.

Toussaint had expected French retaliation but not an armada of such size. "Friends, we must die. The whole of France has come to our island to avenge herself and make us slaves again. Let us at least prove worthy of Liberty," he said as he ordered his army into battle.

Christophe was given the job of defending Cap Français. When he saw that he could not hold out against the invaders, he ordered the people out of the city, and his soldiers put it to the torch. The flames lit the night sky for miles inland. When Leclerc came ashore only 59 of the 2,000 buildings remained usable.

A short time later, Port-au-Prince also fell to the French invaders. Again, the Negro defenders attempted to burn the city, but the French landing was accomplished so swiftly that most of the buildings were saved. Napoleon's intention had been to bring a rich and vital colony back into the French empire, not an island of scorched ruins. His instructions to Leclerc were for four stages for the expedition. First, by flattery and conciliatory measures they were to try to make peace with the Negroes. Second, they were to slowly start enforcing some of Napoleon's demands. Third, either voluntarily or by arrest they were to get Toussaint to France. And fourth, though not written into the plan but by tacit agreement, they were to restore slavery.

To carry out the first phase, Leclerc entered into negotiations with Toussaint. Napoleon had sent Toussaint's two oldest sons along with their French tutor as members of the expedition. In an interview with the boys before they sailed, Napoleon had explained that he intended no harm to their father but hoped only to bring him back into the union with France. A meeting between Toussaint and his sons was arranged. Toussaint was not gulled by Napoleon's offer. Bursting into tears, Isaac, Toussaint's real son, cried that he would never fight against France; but Placide, Toussaint's stepson, threw himself in his father's arms, saying he would stay with him and fight for Haiti to the end.

Though Leclerc appeared to have the advantage in the beginning, the situation soon changed. Toussaint and his men retreated into the mountainous interior, where it was impossible for the French forces to dislodge them. All over Haiti the workers whom Toussaint had sent back to the plantations began to leave the fields to join him. In the first month, Leclerc lost 5,000 men in battle with another 8,000 hospitalized with wounds or yellow fever. More troops landed almost daily only to be swallowed up in battle or by the early arrival of the yellow-fever season.

With his position growing steadily worse, the time seemed to have come for Leclerc to abandon stage one of the plan and move swiftly to stage three. Negotiations were resumed with Toussaint, and he was invited by one of Leclerc's generals to a meeting to talk over terms of peace. For years one of Toussaint's favorite quotations had been "Distrust is the mother of security." Now with the enemy forced into a weakened position and hoping to avert further bloodshed, he forgot his old motto. Accompanied only by Placide and an aide-de-camp, he traveled to a plantation house, where the meeting had been arranged. A French general greeted him cordially, but suddenly excused himself. Moments later a company of soldiers rushed into the room and placed Toussaint under arrest. His hands bound, he was hustled from the house to a waiting carriage and whisked to the coast, where he was put aboard the French frigate *Héros*.

On June 15th, the rest of Toussaint's family having been brought aboard, the *Héros* set sail for Brest. On their arrival in Europe, the members of the family were dispersed to several towns, where they were to live in exile. Warned that Toussaint's execution might cause devastating uprisings in Haiti, Napoleon ordered him locked up in the prison at Jura near the Swiss border, where he was confined in a dark, underground dungeon. Officers were sent to question him in the mistaken belief that somewhere in Haiti he had hidden a great fortune, seized from the whites. When Toussaint failed to supply the answers sought by his questioners, they seemed to forget him.

Accustomed to the warm tropics, Toussaint failed rapidly in the bitter cold of his mountain prison. On April 6, 1803, a jailer entered Toussaint's cell and found him dead in his chair before the cold ashes of his small fireplace. He was buried beneath the floor of the prison chapel in an unmarked grave. Years later, during the course of remodeling, a number of skeletons were found beneath the floor and all were thrown together to become part of the foundations and wall of a new building.

"In overthrowing me they have only felled the tree of Negro liberty in St. Domingo. It will shoot up again, for it is deeply rooted and its roots are many," Toussaint said following his capture.

The prophecy proved true. The yellow fever continued to take its toll of French forces, with General Leclerc himself one of its victims. Beset with continuing wars in Europe, Napoleon abandoned his dream of a colonial empire in the New World. In 1803 he sold the Louisiana Territory to the United States and ordered what remained of the ill-fated expedition, which had cost the lives of 63,000 French soldiers, withdrawn from Haiti.

For two years Dessalines ruled as a despot over independent Haiti. Following his death the country divided, Christophe continuing his despotic rule in the north while a more moderate mulatto leader, Alexandre Pétion, set up a republican government in the south until 1818, when Haiti was reunited as an independent nation.

Later, Spanish Santo Domingo declared its independence from Spain only to be overrun by armies from Haiti, but in 1844 it, too, gained its freedom as a separate country.

Today Toussaint L'Ouverture is honored as Haiti's greatest hero, the slave who led the way for independence in not only Haiti but all of Latin America.

3 ▨ Birth of a Dream

JOSÉ DE SAN MARTÍN, 1778–1814

José de San Martín is honored as the national hero of Argentina; but like that other great South American, Simón Bolívar, his exploits were not limited to a single country. Chile and Peru also claim him as their national hero. Though the Latin American Revolution produced dozens of great leaders, Bolívar and San Martín stand above all the others as South America's two greatest liberators: Bolívar leading the colonies of the north and San Martín leading those of the south in their fight for freedom.

José de San Martín was born on February 25, 1778, in the small Indian village of Yapeyú along the Uruguay River in northeastern Argentina, where his father, a Spanish military officer, was stationed as governor of the surrounding area. The San Martín family belonged to the military elite of that day. San Martín's mother was the daughter of a military man, and his ancestors on both sides, as well as brothers, were soldiers. José, the youngest of a family of four boys and one girl, was also expected to follow a military career.

In spite of the family's seemingly favored position, they were far from wealthy. The work of a frontier governor was demanding and the pay modest. Yapeyú had been founded originally as a Jesuit mission settlement. In 1767, when the Jesuits were expelled from the New World because of their growing power and liberal teachings, the missions passed into military control. Over the centuries, as Portuguese settlers from Brazil pressed south into what are now the countries of

Paraguay and Uruguay, there was conflict with the Spanish settlers to the south. San Martín's father had the dual task of guarding the border against Portuguese expansion and administering the affairs of the large Indian population. The climate of the area was subtropical, supporting orange, lemon, fig, peach, pear, and apple orchards and rich grazing lands. The governor's headquarters were in a commodious, thick-walled building that had once housed the Jesuit school, located across a small plaza from the town church. Though José's father's paycheck frequently arrived late from Buenos Aires, the family lived comfortably off the land.

It was not until 1776, two years before San Martín's birth, that Argentina was made a viceroyalty. For two centuries following the Spanish conquest, Imperial Spain's sole interest in the New World was its mineral wealth. Argentina, with her temperate coastal valleys and her great interior grasslands that reached the base of the towering Andes, was principally an agricultural country. The demand for beef and horses gave the colonists some early industry, but for years Spain pursued the shortsighted policy that all Argentine exports had to be shipped from the port of Lima, Peru, on the Pacific coast. Cattle hides sent to Spain had to be carried 1,500 miles over the 20,000-foot mountains to reach Lima.

Native cattlemen made small profits. Since imports and European luxuries arrived by the same route, their prices were prohibitive except for the wealthy. Smuggling became a common practice along Argentina's long coastline. The great estuary of the Rio de la Plata, with Buenos Aires on the south shore and Montevideo on the north, and its numerous inlets and islands offered ideal landing places for smugglers. The ships that brought contraband goods to Argentina also brought foreign ideas. For years, while Argentina struggled along as the most neglected of Spain's South American colonies, she was also becoming the most liberal and independent. In 1776, when the Viceroyalty of La Plata was created by adding a major portion of Paraguay, Uruguay, and some of the rich silver mines of Bolivia to the former territory of Argentina, the colony began to prosper. Trade was no longer restricted to passage through Lima. The products of Chile and Bolivia began to travel westward across the Andes and Argentina to Buenos Aires, on a new and shorter route to Europe. Within a few years Buenos Aires burgeoned into a bustling seaport. But the changes came too late to alter the spirit of the people. They remained rugged and independent.

San Martín's family saw the beginning of this change. Three years after San Martín's birth, his father was ordered back to Buenos Aires. When San Martín was eight, the family returned to Spain. For San Martín's parents it was a welcome return to their homeland. Of the five children born in the colonies only San Martín would ever return to Argentina.

For three years after the return to Spain, San Martín attended the Nobles' Seminary, an old and aristocratic school for boys in Madrid. He was a solemn boy, diligent and conscientious, but too practical and down-to-earth in his interests to be considered brilliant. Though his father had received a modest increase in salary, the family still found it difficult to maintain a standard of living befitting its station. To ease expenses, San Martín's older brothers had already enlisted in the army. At eleven years of age, San Martín followed their example and applied for admission as a cadet in the Murcia Regiment. His letter of acceptance arrived in July, 1789, the same month that street mobs stormed the Bastille in Paris, launching the French Revolution.

Spain was still struggling to retain her crumbling reputation as a world power. For the next twenty-five years she was almost continually at war, fighting first on one side, then on the other as Charles IV and his vacillating government jockeyed to gain the best advantage for the weakening empire. As a loyal soldier of the king, San Martín fought where he was sent for the next twenty years.

His first battle experience came when he was thirteen, fighting against the Moors in Africa. Next he joined a regiment sent to invade France, so distinguishing himself in the fighting that he was made a lieutenant at eighteen. In 1796, when Charles IV switched loyalties and became a French ally, San Martín fought at sea, aboard a Spanish warship pitted against the British. Later, when Napoleon provoked Spain into a brief and foolish war against Portugal, he saw action in Portugal.

Around 1803, San Martín was stationed briefly at Cádiz. The switch from battle to garrison life gave him leisure he had not had before. Since he was unmarried and little inclined toward social life, he read and improved his education, concentrating on mathematics, military science, geography, and history, subjects that might improve his ability as a military officer.

Located at the southwestern tip of Spain on the Atlantic coast, Cádiz was a bustling port city and the gateway to the New World. Foreign vessels putting into its harbor brought news of the world and an influx of foreign ideas. Through Cádiz also passed the wealthy Creoles of the colonies on their way to and from Madrid. Though the wealth of their mines and plantations supplied Charles IV with the money for his armies, the Creoles themselves had almost no standing as Spanish citizens. In the colonies they were subject to heavy taxation and governing officials sent from Spain. In Spain they were treated as second-class citizens with little chance for advancement in the army or government office.

San Martín was one of the few exceptions. Because his father was a Spaniard and he had lived only a few years in the colonies, he advanced steadily in the army despite his Creole birth. In 1807–8, when Napoleon invaded Portugal, then moved on into Spain, forcing the abdication first of Charles IV, then his son Ferdinand VII, San Martín was called back* to battle, fighting France once again. By 1809 he had been decorated several times and advanced to lieutenant-colonel. But beneath his poised appearance as a loyal Spanish officer, tremendous changes were taking place.

Unlike Simón Bolívar and many of the other Latin American liberators, San Martín did not express his feelings freely. While the others left records of their mounting enthusiasm for colonial independence through speeches, political writings, and correspondence, San Martín was self-contained and inclined to let his actions speak for him. Historians do not know what prompted him to return to South America. We can only guess what his reasons may have been.

San Martín was not given to hasty decisions, so the changes in his thinking must have been going on for some time. He must have felt a growing disillusionment with the vacillating attitude of the Spanish monarchy, which changed sides constantly without consideration for its fighting men. With the abdication of Charles IV and Ferdinand VII, San Martín may have felt that after twenty years of fighting he had fulfilled any obligation to Spain.

Though San Martín sympathized with the basic ideals of the French Revolution, he disapproved of the chaos it had created in Europe. In 1809, while he was serving in Cádiz, he had commanded a small party of soldiers that had held off a rioting street mob attempting to storm his commander's headquarters. The unrestrained frenzy of the mob left a lasting impression on his mind and made San Martín an advocate of strong and orderly government for the rest of his life.

Through his Creole friends, San Martín had learned about the growing movement toward independence that was taking place in Argentina and all of the South American countries. South America appeared to be a land of the future, where new and orderly independent governments might be set up, free of the corruption and chaos of Europe. But the colonies desperately needed soldiers to help in their struggle.

In 1811, at thirty-three years of age, with the possibility of a brilliant military future ahead of him in Europe, San Martín suddenly retired. He gave ill health as his reason, but only a short time later he secured the necessary passport and sailed for England.

London was filled with patriotic Creoles, many of whom had gone to England in the hope of securing British aid in their movement for independence from Spain. After Napoleon's invasion of Spain, Great Britain and Spain had become allies again, thus temporarily dimming this hope, but Creoles continued to hold their discussions. Their meeting place was the former home of Francisco Miranda, a fiery Venezuelan soldier of fortune who had fought in the American and French revolutions, and had made one abortive attempt to land a small revolutionary force in Venezuela. When San Martín arrived, Miranda had already returned to South America to help in Venezuela's fight for freedom, but his home continued to be the headquarters of a secret society known as the Lautaro Lodge, named after a South American Indian youth who had successfully defied his Spanish conquerors during the sixteenth century. Its ritual was patterned after that of the Masonic orders, but its purpose was to secure the independence of Latin America and offer a meeting place for cooperation and assistance between all the colonies. San Martín became a member of the lodge. Early in 1812, with fifty other patriots, he set sail aboard the British frigate *George Channing*, bound for Buenos Aires.

The passage was long and difficult, with passengers subjected to meager diet and rationed water for most of the journey. While it had been little more than a smugglers' haven, Buenos Aires had been a rowdy, ramshackle town, with crude thatch-roofed huts and rutted dirt streets. In the thirty-five years since creation of the Viceroyalty of La Plata had converted it into an active port, some improvements had been made. Public buildings and a cathedral had been built and some of the streets had been paved, but it still resembled a raw frontier town.

For the colonists of Argentina the move toward self-government had come earlier than it had in the other colonies. In 1806, while Spain was still allied with the French, a British expeditionary force had attempted to seize Buenos Aires and Montevideo. When the Spanish viceroy failed to protect the colonists, they united under a French sea captain, Santiago de Liniers, and repulsed the invaders themselves. Jubilant over their victory, they ordered the viceroy home and Charles IV allowed Liniers to remain in power as the new viceroy. In time, as feeling turned against France, Liniers was replaced, but the colonists had tested their own military strength and had enjoyed the right to choose their own leaders. On May 25, 1810, after receiving news of the abdications of Charles IV and Ferdinand VII and Napoleon's invasion of France, Argentina's colonists formed a *junta*, or council, of their own to rule until the monarchy could be restored. Like the in-

dependent governments set up in the other colonies at the
same time, they did not make a clean break with the mother
country but continued to profess loyalty to Ferdinand VII,
should he be restored to the throne. In spite of the colonial
governments' professions of loyalty, the Spanish government
was suspicious. By opening their ports to foreign trade, freeing their slaves, and instituting new laws, the colonies appeared to be moving toward total independence. When San
Martín reached Buenos Aires in 1812, Argentina was the
only one of the independent governments that had not been
overthrown or was not in the process of being overthrown by
Spanish military forces.

Since it was founded as an agricultural colony, Argentina's
population and culture had developed along lines different
from those of the other colonies. The traditional Spanish
colonial system that resulted in the establishment of an
enormously wealthy landowning class contrasted to an impoverished slave or laboring class was not as firmly entrenched
in Argentina. Around Buenos Aires, in particular, white merchants and the owners of small farms and ranches made
Argentina the one colony with a sizable educated middle
class. Racism was also less prevalent in Argentina. Slavery
had never flourished as it had in many of the other colonies.
It was relatively simple for the slaves of Argentina to escape
from their coastal areas and flee into the interior, where their
owners seldom bothered to pursue them. Black, Indian, and
white races intermarried freely, and a year before San Martín's
arrival, slavery had been abolished.

In spite of its liberal policies, Argentina's independent government was beset with internal problems. The colonists of
Paraguay and Uruguay, under local patriots of their own, had
sought to break away. In Buenos Aires, the government was

split into quarreling factions, some conservative and still loyal to Spain, others desiring complete independence. Overconfident of the military ability of her army after the British were repelled, Argentina sent a large force of soldiers, under the able general Manuel Belgrano, north along the old supply route to Lima to secure the Bolivian mining area that had been added to the Viceroyalty of La Plata and, optimistically, to assist in the liberation of Peru. Belgrano won victories at first, but as his supply lines were stretched thinner and thinner and he met increasingly larger forces from Peru, he began to suffer reverses.

Perhaps the most serious problem faced by the new government was Argentina's geography and vast size. Two thousand miles long and over 800 miles wide at its widest portion, Argentina was the largest Spanish colony of the New World. Also, it was divided into areas where the culture and way of life of the people were very different. Along the coast and extending for some distance up the Rio de La Plata and its tributaries, the climate was subtropical. In this region were concentrated the merchants and a majority of small-ranch and farm owners.

Immediately behind Buenos Aires and sprawling for miles across the interior of Argentina were the *pampas*, or grasslands. Ranches fringed the eastern edge nearest the coast, but the vast interior with its herds of wild cattle, sprung from runaway stock of the early settlers, was the home of the nomadic *gauchos*. These South American "cowboys" were a polyglot of mixed races. They were wild, rugged, unsurpassed as horsemen, and led by local chieftains who distrusted the city dwellers to the east.

Farther west, at the base of the Andes, the country changed again. Rich alluvial plains fanned down from the mountains, and the land was broken up into farms and ranches again. In scattered cities with great cathedrals and manorial homes, people clung to the old colonial ways, with large land holdings worked by Indian laborers. Here ideas and interests tended to be more conservative. For the struggling government at Buenos Aires it was virtually impossible to please, let alone control, such a diverse population.

San Martín arrived in Buenos Aires when he was thirty-four years of age. He was of average height and looks, and had an unmistakable military bearing. Years of outdoor life had darkened his olive complexion so that he might have been mistaken for an Indian. He was lean, rawboned, with straight black hair always worn short, a long, straight nose, and deep-set, dark eyes that gave his inferiors the uncomfortable sensation that he saw their innermost thoughts. Because he did not give passionate speeches about his patriotism and had once been a Spanish soldier, he was viewed at first with suspicion by some of the Creoles. He was not offered a command in the existing army, but was given permission to raise a cavalry regiment of his own. For his headquarters he chose an abandoned slave market, El Ribero, near the river. The crude shed-like buildings had fallen into disrepair and the former auction square had been converted into a bull ring. San Martín used the buildings for his barracks, while the bull ring became his drill ground. In spite of these modest training quarters, hundreds of young men, drawn by San Martín's military reputation, joined his grenadiers. San Martín screened them carefully, making the Creoles his officers and the gauchos and laborers his regular soldiers.

He was a tireless and exacting taskmaster. He drilled his troops for hours on end in the manner of the French cavalry, stressing the use of the long, curved saber favored by Napo-

JOSÉ DE SAN MARTÍN

leon's forces. He often routed his men out of bed in the middle of the night for exercises. In Buenos Aires, San Martín had joined a newly organized branch of the Lautaro Lodge. His officers were also made members and all of his soldiers were indoctrinated in its goals to secure freedom for the people of Argentina and offer assistance to all the other colonies of South America engaged in the same struggle. San Martín had such ability as a military leader that in time this one regiment of grenadiers would contribute 19 generals and 200 officers to the cause of Latin American independence. When the last battle for independence was over, only 7 men of the original regiment were alive to return to their families and accept the honors waiting for them.

In spite of the Spartan living conditions he imposed on himself and his soldiers, San Martín occasionally attended some of the social functions given by the city's Creole families. Soon most of these rare idle hours were spent at the home of wealthy and influential Don Antonio de Escalada. Five months after San Martín arrived at Buenos Aires, he was granted the necessary military permission to marry Maria Remedios Escalada, Escalada's fifteen-year-old daughter. The wedding took place on September 12, 1812, in the Cathedral of Buenos Aires.

The couple seemed oddly mismatched because of the great difference in their ages. Maria Remedios' principal attributes as a bride were considered to be her pretty face, extremely small feet (a mark of gentility in those days), and her family's wealth. But she shared San Martín's dream of freedom for all of South America. He had already begun a practice he would continue throughout the revolution, contributing half of his salary toward the purchase of arms for his men. In June, two months before the wedding, when the wealthy young women of the city were urged to sign a pledge donating money to the cause, Maria Remedios' name was first on the list. She was to become San Martín's confidant, helper, and strongest supporter.

The government had fallen into the hands of a reactionary triumvirate, or ruling body of three men. They had failed to furnish adequate support to General Belgrano's armies and delayed calling a general assembly. Members of the Lautaro Lodge plotted a military coup to force a more liberal government. On October 7, 1812, San Martín and his grenadiers joined other military units surrounding the town hall on the Plaza Victoria. They rang the tower bell, Argentina's liberty bell, summoning the people. Soon the crowd had swollen to about 2,000. San Martín accompanied several local leaders into the hall, where they demanded the appointment of a new triumvirate. While the council then in session debated the matter, the crowd grew restive. San Martín remembered the mob at Cádiz. He warned the council to make its decision before the crowd made it. The warning was sufficient; the council gave in and ordered the removal of the three reactionary leaders.

The new government immediately ordered elections and the summoning of a national assembly that would more equally represent all areas of the country. San Martín's part in the coup allayed some of the suspicions about his loyalty to Argentina.

By early 1813, Buenos Aires was swept with a new alarm. A flotilla of Spanish warships had put into the wide mouth of the Rio de la Plata, apparently with the intention of landing north of the city. Because Belgrano's forces were fighting far to the north, San Martín's grenadiers were to repulse the attack.

San Martín immediately left the city at the head of 120 cavalrymen. Seventeen miles up the Paraná River, which joins the Rio de la Plata only a short distance north of Buenos Aires, was the tiny village of San Lorenzo, with a thick-walled Franciscan monastery on the bluffs overlooking both the village and the river. San Martín led his horsemen through the back gates of the monastery, ordering them to remain hidden behind the walls. Disguised in the poncho and wide sombrero of an Indian farmer, he rode alone along the bank of the river, where he watched eleven Spanish warships move slowly up the river, drop anchor, and begin preparations to put soldiers ashore.

Galloping back to the monastery, San Martín ordered his men to remain in hiding and to keep their mounts quiet so no betraying dust might rise above the walls. From the convent tower he continued to watch the movements of the Spaniards. They had field artillery and about 300 well-armed marines and infantrymen. San Martín's men had no artillery, and many were armed only with sabers or pikes.

San Martín counted on their discipline and the element of surprise. He let the Spaniards land and move well inland. Then, ordering the monks to throw open the gate, he led his men out of the monastery and down the slopes on their fast Argentine ponies. So quickly was the charge executed that within minutes both sides were in hand-to-hand combat. San Martín, who was in the lead, locked sabers with the advancing Spanish commander. Later in the melee of the close-quarter fighting, they were separated, but the Spaniards had managed to draw up one cannon. San Martín's horse was shot from under him in the first shrapnel round, pinning him to the ground by one leg. Blood was already running down his face from a saber wound in the cheek, and a Spanish infantryman rushed forward to finish him off. Two of San Martín's soldiers rushed forward, one killing the Spaniard with his lance and the other dragging his commander free of the fallen horse. On foot San Martín charged back into the battle.

Within a short time victory was assured. The Spaniards began retreating toward the river, leaving behind two cannon, many arms, and 40 dead companions. San Martín's losses had been 15 dead and 27 wounded. Without cleaning the blood from his face and uniform, San Martín returned to the monastery where, seated beneath a pine tree, he wrote the dispatches telling of his first victory for Argentina.

The battle at San Lorenzo in February, 1813, ended the threat of Spanish attacks on the river ports. San Martín returned to Buenos Aires a hero. Suspicion about his loyalty had vanished. But the city's air of jubilation lasted only a few months, as it began to receive reports of the increasingly severe defeats General Belgrano was suffering in the north. San Martín was ordered north to take over reorganization of Belgrano's army.

The 800 mile journey to his new command was arduous and time consuming, and San Martín did not arrive until the end of the year. Long before he reached his new headquarters at Tucumán in northwestern Argentina, he realized the folly of trying to maintain an army over such a long supply route. Tucumán was little more than a hospital city, filled to overflowing with the wounded, half-starved, and demoralized soldiers who straggled back in small groups from their rout on the Bolivian battlefields in the north. Belgrano and San Martín formed a friendship on sight. Belgrano immediately offered to turn over his command, but San Martín refused. The final decision was taken out of their hands. Belgrano was called back to Buenos Aires to stand trial for his defeats, and San Martín was ordered to take over his position.

As the soldiers recovered, San Martín drilled and trained

Rescue of San Martín at San Lorenzo

them as he had his grenadiers. Gradually, Tucumán began to look like a vast training camp. In Buenos Aires, other generals were jealous of San Martín's rapid advancement. Soon even government officials became restless. They had sent San Martín

north in expectation of victories in Bolivia, not endless training. Adding to their uneasiness was the latest news from Europe. Napoleon had been defeated and Ferdinand VII had been restored to the throne. Spanish soldiers, freed from fighting on the continent, were being sent to South America to put down rebellion in the colonies. Argentina was stirred to a foment of haste and urgency. Other generals insisted that Spanish troops already on South American soil must be defeated before reinforcements arrived.

In spite of repeated messages from Buenos Aires, San Martín refused to be hurried or provoked into hasty action. He had disapproved of the campaign in Bolivia, and the months in Tucumán had reinforced his conviction that it had little chance for success. He asked to be relieved of his command. Once again he used ill health as his reason. The excuse was not without foundation. After twenty-five years of the strenuous life of a soldier, he suffered from stomach ulcers, arthritis so crippling that at times he had to be lifted onto his horse, and was showing early symptoms of tuberculosis. He asked to be reassigned to the relatively minor post of governor of Cuyo (now Mendoza), a remote province almost due west of Buenos Aires at the base of the Andes, along the Chilean border.

The request was granted and by September, 1814, San Martín had reached Mendoza, the capital city of Cuyo. Maria Remedios, now eighteen years old, made the long, perilous journey across the *pampas* by stagecoach to join him. The high, dry climate of Cuyo was considered particularly healthful, but this was not what had prompted San Martín to ask for the assignment. He had a scheme so daring that until he convinced others of its feasibility he dared not reveal it.

4 ⊠ Warrior of the Andes

JOSÉ DE SAN MARTÍN, 1815–1850

San Martín had reached the same conclusion that Simón Bolívar, fighting for the colonies in the north, was also reaching. As long as Peru, the richest of Spain's colonies, remained a stronghold from which the Spaniards could outfit troops and send them either north or south, none of the independent colonies could ever hope for permanent peace. The conquest of Peru promised to be a formidable task. Centuries earlier Argentine cattlemen had discovered the difficulties of taking their hides 3,000 miles northwest across the Bolivian Andes to the port of Lima. It would be folly to believe Argentina could supply an army over such a distance, particularly while the Spanish forces of Peru were being reinforced easily by sea. However, the town of Mendoza, situated at the foot of the Andes, lay almost directly opposite Valparaiso, Chile, where the young Chilean patriot Bernardo O'Higgins was leading his countrymen in a similar struggle for independence. If San Martín could get his troops over the Andes, they could help Chile secure her independence. Then, supplied from Chile and reinforced by O'Higgins' Chilean army, they could sail north to attack Peru at her most vulnerable point, along the seacoast from which she received her supplies from Spain.

The Andes, 20,000 feet high, with only narrow zigzag trails leading to the high passes of Uspallata, Los Patos, and La Plancha, were San Martín's most serious obstacle. With the determined thoroughness with which he undertook every enterprise, he outfitted and trained an army for the assault.

The plan was so audacious that in the beginning only Maria Remedios and a few of San Martín's friends knew what he had in mind. Once he arrived in Mendoza the secret could not be kept for long. Many of the townspeople supported him from the beginning. As their enthusiasm grew it spread to the others. To save money, San Martín refused to live in the lavish provincial palace. One-half of his salary was used to equip the army. From the surrounding plains men flocked to join his forces. Farmers offered supplies and horses. San Martín's wife set an example for the wealthy women of the town by donating her jewels to raise money. Later she helped organize the women in the task of carding, dying, spinning, and sewing llama wool and goat hair into sturdy blue uniforms designed to protect the soldiers against the cold of the high altitudes.

The cause received its greatest boost when a quiet, brown-robed Franciscan friar, Fray Luis Beltrán, arrived in Mendoza to offer his services. Behind his self-effacing exterior, Beltrán was a mechanical genius and master craftsman in almost every field. There seemed to be nothing he could not design, build, or manufacture. Under his direction, forges were set up for casting cannon, and making cutlasses, swords, pikes, and 50,-000 horseshoes to support horses and pack animals over the rocky trails. He set up factories to make ammunition, fashion saddles and bridles, and grind dried beef into a powder called *charqui*, which would serve as the basic field ration.

"If the cannons need wings, they shall have them," Beltrán said, and he designed portable bridges, some of them 175 feet long with gigantic iron spikes that would anchor them across mountain chasms. He designed special narrow wagons that could traverse the rocky trails.

Meanwhile, San Martín drilled his soldiers, planned with his officers, and drilled his soldiers again. He asked no more of his men than he demanded of himself. He rose early and after a frugal breakfast turned immediately to the work of the day. Occasionally at midday he permitted himself a brief nap on a cot set up in the corridor of his headquarters, but after a modest dinner he often worked far into the night.

At the same time that he was drilling troops and manufacturing and gathering supplies at Mendoza, he stationed men in the mountains to study the trails and the terrain over which they had to pass. One day a courier galloped into Mendoza with dismaying news. In Chile the republican troops of Bernardo O'Higgins had been defeated. Those who had managed to escape were struggling across the Andes to reach San Martín.

San Martín ordered pack trains into the mountains to meet the straggling, half-starved men with blankets, food, and clothing. He accompanied one of the trains himself. When he and O'Higgins met, they dismounted and embraced, forming from that moment a lifelong friendship.

O'Higgins was six months younger than San Martín, of medium height and somewhat stocky build, with a round, animated, boyish face. He wore his dark curly hair cut short but affected long sideburns that curled almost to his chin, in an effort to minimize his plump cheeks and look more mature. Where San Martín's face was inclined to be grave and his dark eyes probing, O'Higgins was sunny and expressive, his eyes constantly dancing.

O'Higgins was the illegitimate son of a former viceroy of Peru. His father, Ambrosio O'Higgins, had gone to Chile as an itinerant peddler, made a fortune, and for supplying Spanish troops, had been appointed first captain-general of Chile and later viceroy of Peru. During his service in Chile he formed a liaison with a young woman from a respected

BERNARDO O'HIGGINS

Creole family, but government regulations forbade their marriage. By the time Bernardo was seventeen, his father had become viceroy of Peru, and the existence of an illegitimate son threatened to be an embarrassment to his high position. Young Bernardo was sent to Europe to be educated, first to Spain, then to England. In London, the lonely youth joined the Lautaro Lodge and became one of the Creoles who met regularly at the home of Francisco Miranda. Here, like the others, he was fired with the desire to free his homeland.

It was not until 1802, after his father's death, that Bernardo returned home, where he found that his father had left him enormous land holdings in Chile as well as the right to abandon his mother's family name of Riquelme and to assume the name O'Higgins. During the following years O'Higgins managed his large estates, but attended the meetings of other patriot Creoles in a new branch of the Lautaro Lodge.

In May, 1810, after learning that Napoleon had invaded Spain, Argentina formed her first independent government. It took longer for the news of Napoleon's invasions to reach across the Andes, but on September 18, 1810, Chile followed suit, replacing the captain-general with a *junta* of local leaders. O'Higgins, an active participant in the move, organized and outfitted two regiments of soldiers to fight for the cause and was elected representative from his district to the first assembly. But Chile, like so many of the other governments, was torn with dissension. When Spanish soldiers were sent south from Peru to put down the rebellion, the quarreling leaders tried too late to patch up their differences. When O'Higgins failed to receive expected reinforcements at the city of Rancagua, his army of 1,500 was defeated. With only 500 men, he escaped from the burning city and over the mountains.

Back at Cuyo, San Martín ordered a special camp set up for the Chileans and named O'Higgins his next in command. Two men could not have been more different in temperament. San Martín was disciplined and methodical; O'Higgins, fiery tempered and impulsive. They complemented each other perfectly. San Martín provided the steadying influence O'Higgins needed, while O'Higgins provided the aggressive right arm San Martín needed in leading troops into battle, particularly as his own health continued to fail.

The two men worked tirelessly, drilling their soldiers during the daylight hours and conducting classes in military tactics at night. San Martín also impressed on his men the need for religious faith. Sunday attendance at Mass was compulsory. Every night, prayers were recited just before taps.

While San Martín labored at Mendoza, other patriots worked to shore up the shaky government in Buenos Aires. Even the most conservative Creoles had become disenchanted with Ferdinand VII. On his return to the throne, Ferdinand had promised a more liberal government both in Spain and the colonies. But within a short time he abolished all reforms enacted in his absence and sent troops to enforce the old colonial system in the colonies. No longer willing to profess allegiance to a tyrannical king, Argentina announced the formation of the Argentine Republic, on July 9, 1816.

Leaving O'Higgins in charge at Mendoza, San Martín rode east to confer with Juan Pueyrredón, head of the new republic. He received Pueyrredón's wholehearted support for his plan of crossing the Andes. When he returned to Mendoza he brought with him the title of "General of the Army of the Andes," as well as Argentina's new blue and white flag.

Crossing the 20,000-foot backbone of the continent continued to be San Martín's principal worry. "What spoils my sleep is not the strength of the enemy, but how to pass these immense mountains," he said. He spent a part of every day poring over his maps.

Finally he arranged for a brilliant young engineer to cross the Andes, carrying the text of Argentina's Declaration of Independence to the Spanish general who now held Chile. It was a dangerous errand, for there was the chance the courier would be killed; but there was a more important reason for the mission. San Martín cared little whether the Spaniards read the Declaration of Independence or not, but he desperately needed information about the area they must travel. The engineer crossed the Andes by one pass, convinced the Spanards he was just an ignorant courier, and returned by another pass. Seated at a table in San Martín's headquarters, he drew from his prodigious memory a complete map of the route they were to follow.

Near the end of 1816, at the time of year when the mountains of the Southern Hemisphere carried the lightest burden of snow, San Martín attended to the final details of the plan to which he had already devoted two years of preparation. When the 5,000 soldiers needed extra blankets, a plea went out to every farm family of Cuyo to donate one blanket. When there were not enough trumpets, an order went to the coast to send more. It was discovered at the last moment that Fray Beltrán's forges had turned out 130 swords too many. A cry went out for volunteers, and a man was found to carry every sword.

Despite his strict discipline and devotion to detail, San Martín was well liked by his men. He appeared to be aloof and unapproachable, but stories about men who had had personal contact with him circulated through the barracks. A favorite tale concerned a promising young officer who, in a moment of weakness, had gambled away a sum of money belonging to his regiment. He appeared before San Martín voluntarily, expecting the worst. In his extreme nervousness, he addressed his petition for an audience to *Citizen* San Martín instead of *General* San Martín.

When San Martín had heard his confession, he took enough

gold coins from a drawer to cover the young officer's embezzlement. "Here is enough gold to cover your losses." Speaking as *Citizen* San Martín, he handed the trembling officer the money. "But be certain you never let *General* San Martín hear about this. He would have you executed on the spot," he warned.

The army was ready in January, 1817. "To the first shot fired beyond the Andes against the oppressors of Chile." San Martín raised a toast at a final banquet with his officers. The soldiers paraded for a last review before the people of Mendoza on streets strewn with flowers. San Martín unfurled their flag. It was blue and white, showing a rising sun and two hands lifting a red liberty cap over the mountain crests. "This is the first independent flag to be blessed in America, soldiers," San Martín said. "Swear to protect it and die in its defense."

"We swear! We swear!" was the thundering reply of the assembled soldiers.

San Martín knew the Spaniards must be aware of his intentions. Shortly before the departure of his troops he visited an Indian village high in the mountains, taking with him many mule loads of presents and asking permission of the chiefs for his army to cross their territory. As he had expected, the Indians told the Spaniards that San Martín's men planned to cross the mountains through La Plancha Pass, expecting gifts from the Spaniards also for the information. San Martín sent a token force into that area, but the main divisions of his army headed directly for the two higher passes, Los Patos and Uspallata. In all, they had about 5,000 men and 9,000 animals. O'Higgins led one of the divisions, traveling by way of Uspallata Pass. San Martín, who was suffering from arthritis, followed behind with the last division.

In places the trails were no more than slippery ledges carved from sheer rock cliffs. Cannon and heavy equipment had to be laboriously swung over chasms and hauled up rocky slopes by cable. In the 12,000-foot altitudes of the passes, both men and animals were stricken with mountain sickness caused by lack of oxygen. Animals slipped from the rocky trails by the hundreds or died of exhaustion. In one place the trail caved away, dropping 50 soldiers 1,000 feet to their death. By the eighteenth day, they had reached the crest of the mountains. As the men made their way across the high, barren plateaus on top of the Andes, icy winds, hailstorms, and below-zero temperatures added to their misery.

More than two-thirds of their animals perished on the crossing. But the warm clothing sewn by the women of Mendoza, the sturdy boots fashioned in the leather factories of Fray Beltrán, and the supplies of *charqui*, which, mixed with cornmeal and boiling water, furnished a nourishing, hot mush, brought most of the men through the mountains safely.

San Martín's planning had been so perfect and his men were so well trained that the groups traveling by the two different passes arrived at their meeting point at exactly the same time. San Martín's decoy efforts had drawn away the main strength of the Spaniards, but now he learned that part of their army was camped near the town of Chacabuco, while reserves alerted to his arrival were rushing to join them from Chile's capital, Santiago.

Before these two units could unite, San Martín ordered a forced night march. At two o'clock on the morning of February 12, his soldiers swarmed out of the mountains into the camp at Chacabuco. The fighting raged throughout the morning with neither side gaining an advantage until shortly after midday, when O'Higgins drove a wedge through the Span-

San Martín and his troops crossing the Andes

iards' strongest defenses, uniting with the grenadiers coming in from the other side. With his army cut in two, the Spanish general ordered a retreat to Santiago.

The exuberant O'Higgins wished to pursue the enemy, but believing his men had reached the limit of their endurance San Martín ordered a brief rest. Soon couriers arrived from Santiago with word that the Spaniards had deserted the capital, and the city was in the hands of looting street mobs. San Martín sent 200 cavalrymen to restore order, while he and the rest of the army followed. In Santiago, San Martín and O'Higgins were given a tumultuous greeting, with church bells ringing and people leaning from balconies to shower them with flowers. When San Martín called an assembly of the leading citizens to form a new government, the crowds began to chant his name, wanting him to take over as their leader. San Martín refused the honor. He had never entertained political ambitions. As a soldier, he had only one commitment, to see all of South America liberated.

O'Higgins lacked San Martín's depth of vision. Though he agreed with the premise that Peru must be defeated if there was to be lasting peace, O'Higgins was a Chilean first, a South American second. When the people learned that San Martín would not accept public office, they gave O'Higgins the office of supreme director of Chile.

For more than a week the citizens of Santiago celebrated their freedom. San Martín and O'Higgins were entertained at a banquet where the entree consisted of roast turkeys served with their heads still attached and gilded, each bearing a small flag of liberation in its beak. San Martín was rewarded with a purse of gold, but he returned the money to the city with orders that it be used to build a public library.

The capital had been liberated, but that did not mean that

Chile was free. The Spanish army held most of southern Chile along with isolated areas in the north, but the liberation of Peru was becoming an obsession with San Martín. He and O'Higgins had already agreed that a Chilean navy should be assembled at Valparaiso to carry on the expedition by sea. Before the end of the victory celebrations, San Martín slipped out of the city with only two companions to head back over the Andes, first to Mendoza, then on to Buenos Aires to confer with Pueyrredón. Still a struggling republic, Argentina did not have many resources to support San Martín's request for ships. But Pueyrredón promised to collect what money he could and to send an emissary to try to purchase vessels in the United States.

Before the end of the year San Martín had rejoined O'Higgins in Chile. Feeling cheated because he had slipped away from the earlier victory celebrations, the Chileans tried to shower San Martín with gifts. He refused most and donated the rest to charity.

Sometimes he grew short-tempered, particularly if he suspected the donors were trying to win his favor. When a known royalist presented San Martín's tailor with an expensive bolt of cloth to make the general some new uniforms, San Martín angrily returned the cloth to the tailor with orders to make the royalist seven new suits instead, with further instructions that the chagrined donor was to put on a new suit each day of the week, walk past San Martín's lodgings, and make a low bow to the windows.

Even the government felt his scorn when they ordered him a fine set of silver service and a salary of 6,000 pesos a year so that he could maintain a living standard befitting his rank. San Martín refused both, with a critical note saying it was not a time for luxuries and the new government could find better use for its limited funds. While he was in the capital, San Martín continued to live frugally. He maintained a state dining room, where he entertained public officials and conferred with his generals; but he usually rose at four each morning and prepared his own breakfast. In the evening, if he did not have dinner guests, he ate standing up in the kitchen.

During San Martín's absence from Chile, things had gone badly for O'Higgins' forces. Reinforced by sea, the Spanish army in the south refused to be dislodged. To bolster the morale of the people, the government proclaimed Chile's independence from Spain on February 12, 1818, and Chile joined the growing list of South American republics.

Boosting morale was not enough. A month later, San Martín and O'Higgins' combined forces met a crushing defeat at Cancha Rayada, just outside of Valparaiso. In the fighting, O'Higgins' horse was shot from under him and his right arm was shattered. As the patriots broke ranks and milled in confusion, Spanish soldiers surrounded San Martín. His aide was killed at his side but with what seemed to be superhuman strength, San Martín slashed his way out of the circle and swam to safety across a nearby river. Defeated and despondent, with O'Higgins barely able to sit in the saddle because of his wounds, they retreated to San Fernando, San Martín's headquarters. There was little doubt that O'Higgins' wounds would keep him out of action for weeks, but San Martín refused to be dismayed, as many of their men escaped the enemy and straggled into camp. Their greatest loss had been their artillery. Once again Fray Beltrán came to San Martín's aid. "Conscript the workers and I'll replace every gun," he promised.

A more serious problem came when news of the defeat reached Santiago. Rumors swept the capital that both O'Hig-

gins and San Martín had been killed. In panic some people
began to pack their belongings to flee the city. Others ran
through the streets shouting "Long live the King!" hoping
this would save their property when the Spaniards arrived.

Though ill with a high fever, O'Higgins rode to the capital
to quiet the people and resume control of the government.
The following day San Martín followed. He was greeted by
the ringing of church bells. In one of his rare public addresses,
he told the crowd, "I pledge my word of honor I shall soon
give a day of glory for all South America."

San Martín kept that pledge less than two weeks later, on
April 5, 1818, when he assembled his forces to meet the
Spaniards at Maipú, 7 miles southeast of Santiago. San Martín would have preferred more time to reorganize, but he had
no choice, as the Spaniards, flushed with the victory at
Cancha Rayada, marched north on the capital. Moreover, he
had to fight without the aid of O'Higgins. What San Martín
did not know was that the Spanish commander had already
committed a tactical blunder. Though the Spaniards had won
the field at Cancha Rayada, their losses and disorganization
had been as great as that of the patriots. Against his staff's
advice to take time out to reorganize, the Spanish commander had directed his weary men north, intent on pursuing the victory.

San Martín had already set up his defenses at Maipú. His
men were issued an extra supply of 100 bullets apiece, a
flagon of *aguardiente*, a fiery liquor strong enough to activate
a mummy, and orders not to fire until the enemy was within
50 paces of their position. "The battle will decide the fate of
all America and it is preferable to suffer an honorable death
on the field of honor than to meet it at the hands of execu-
tioners. . . ." San Martín told them.

The battle was one of the bloodiest yet fought on South American soil and an overwhelming victory for the patriots. Two thousand Spanish soldiers were slain, another 2,000 taken prisoner. As the remainder fled for the coast and their ships, San Martín called a halt to the massacre.

In Santiago, O'Higgins had refused to remain in his sick bed. Riding out from the city, he climbed a small hill just in time to witness the rout of the enemy. Unmindful of his injuries, he galloped onto the field of battle, leaped from his horse, and embraced San Martín with his good arm. "Glory, glory to the savior of Chile," he cried.

In his haste to escape capture, the Spanish commander had been forced to abandon his carriage. Inside, one of San Martín's aides found a portfolio of secret papers. Many of them were letters from leading citizens of Santiago who, after the defeat at Cancha Rayada, had written to offer to return their allegiance to Spain in order to save their lives and estates. Drawing aside, San Martín read each letter grimly, then ordered the entire portfolio burned. Aware that Chile would need the help of even these cowardly citizens in her job of reconstruction, San Martín never revealed the names, least of all to the hot-tempered O'Higgins.

The battle of Maipú freed Chile. Except for minor operations, the Spanish army had been driven permanently from Chilean soil. San Martín was free to turn his attention to the Peruvian campaign. Once again he went back over the Andes to confer with the government of Argentina. He was promised financial support, but the government was never able to raise more than a small part of the promised funds.

Meanwhile, in Chile, O'Higgins had undertaken the task of gathering the navy that was to take the invasion forces

San Martín and O'Higgins at the Battle of Maipú in Chile

north. The Argentine emissary to the United States had found sympathy for his cause but little aid. By seizure and purchase, O'Higgins acquired several small ships, which he re-outfitted as gunboats. Learning that eleven Spanish merchantmen protected by an escort of three armed vessels had rounded the Horn and were heading for Peru, O'Higgins sent four of his gunboats to intercept them. "With four little ships, Spain discovered the New World and won a great empire. With four ships, we shall take it away from her," he told those who scoffed at his effort.

The Chilean gunboats were successful, and soon Chile boasted a navy of sixteen vessels. The greatest boost to the building of the navy came when O'Higgins secured the services of a renegade British naval officer, Lord Thomas Cochrane, whose reputation was little better than that of a pirate. Cochrane's services were not cheap, but he agreed to sail along the South American coast, seizing other vessels, keeping the cargo for himself, and bringing the vessels into Chilean ports to be re-outfitted for the navy.

San Martín's transportation problem appeared to be solved; but no sooner was one crisis met than another took its place. In Argentina, the government once again was torn with dissension. Word came from Spain that Ferdinand was preparing a mammoth expeditionary force of 20,000 soldiers to put down the revolt in the colonies. In time it was revealed that the actual goal of this invasion force was Venezuela, but the warning caused a fresh outbreak of panic in Argentina. Pueyrredón was forced to resign in favor of a new leader, and San Martín received orders to return home with Argentina's army. San Martín returned to Mendoza, but with only a small force of soldiers. "I would have wasted my army of invasion in a welter of confusion," he later explained.

Argentina's new government was displeased. Realizing he could expect no more help from that quarter, San Martín sent his wife and young daughter, Mercedes, to Buenos Aires and resigned as commander of the Argentine army. Still committed to carrying the fight to Peru, but no longer holding military title, he returned to Chile. His health was so poor he had to be carried most of the way on a litter. O'Higgins rode out to meet him with a great parade of their combined soldiers. Before they entered the capital, O'Higgins had given San Martín the rank of brigadier general of the Chilean army.

Most of the soldiers of the Army of the Andes voted to defy their own government and remain with San Martín for the conquest of Peru. San Martín's action brought denunciations from Argentina. No longer a public hero, he was accused of treachery and of being bribed by the Chileans. "It seems revolutions open a vast field of malevolence and that it is chiefly directed against those who have the misfortune to command. . . ." he wrote in reply.

Delays and bickering had cost San Martín two years since the victory at Maipú, but on August 20, 1820, his invasion fleet of eight war vessels, sixteen transports, around 5,000 men and enough supplies to last six months set sail from Valparaiso. Lord Cochrane's activities along the coast had already bottled up most of the Spanish ships in the harbor of Callao, the port city for Peru's capital of Lima. Cochrane wanted to open a frontal assault directly on the city, but San Martín ordered his troops put ashore to the south in preparation for a lengthy seige. "Remember that you come not as conquerors, but as liberators. The Peruvians are our brothers," he cautioned his men.

It was a waiting game that took almost a year. Cochrane's ships maintained a blockade, keeping Lima from receiving supplies by sea. San Martín's troops cut off other supplies by land. Morale crumbled inside the city. Defectors slipped away to join the patriots. But San Martín's forces suffered from the inactivity also. Many deserted while others died of malaria.

In the end San Martín's patience triumphed. The Spanish viceroy withdrew with his army toward the Andes. On July 10, 1821, quietly and accompanied by only one aide, San Martín slipped into the city at the invitation of the leading citizens. In spite of his efforts at secrecy, he was recognized as he entered the viceregal palace. "Long live the general!" the cry went up from the people who were rapidly assembling.

"No! Long live the Independence of Peru!" San Martín corrected.

San Martín called a meeting of the local council, and on July 28, 1821, Peru officially declared her independence. The red and gold flag of Spain was replaced with the red and white flag of Peru. The city celebrated for three days with street parades, tolling bells, volleys of gunfire, and nightly fireworks. Today Peru still celebrates her independence with a three-day holiday beginning on July 28th.

The local council immediately voted to make San Martín head of the new government. This time he had no one like O'Higgins, whom he could trust with the position. He chose the title, "Protector of Peru," an office that gave him leadership until Peru was completely free and ready to establish her own government. The decision brought problems that he had never faced before.

The situation in Peru was similar to that which had existed in Chile. The capital had been freed, but the Spanish army had not been defeated. However, in Peru royalist sentiment was much stronger than it had been in Chile. While many of the leading citizens appeared to support San Martín, they secretly opposed him. The wealth of Peru's mines had created an enormously wealthy Creole class in contrast to an impoverished laboring class of Indians and mestizos. Many Creoles feared that republicanism might destroy their power.

Instead of getting on with his military plans, San Martín found his time taken up with government problems. As a military man he had always been a strong disciplinarian. It was the only way he knew how to rule, but when he assumed this same strict approach in government, the people accused him of being a dictator. There were false rumors that he secretly planned to make himself king.

The citizens of Peru were not the only ones becoming restless. Back in Chile, O'Higgins' government was running into trouble. Once their country was freed, the people of Chile, like those of Argentina, began to resent heavy taxes to support an army on foreign soil. In Peru, more soldiers deserted. Lord Cochrane demanded payment for the service of his ships. When San Martín was unable to meet his demands, he sailed off in a huff with most of the fleet.

San Martín, once a man of energy, began to suffer from spells of lethargy. However, he clung to his conviction that the last Spanish soldier had to be driven from South American soil. He knew now that he could not defeat the Spanish forces without help. Argentina and Chile had already been drained to the limit. To the north, another army of liberation, led by a Venezuelan, Simón Bolívar, was moving slowly toward Peru, after freeing Venezuela, Colombia, and Ecuador. San Martín realized that only with Bolívar's help could the final victory be won. Letters passed between the two leaders, and the Ecuadorian port of Guayaquil was selected for a meeting.

One of the finest ports on the Pacific coast, Guayaquil had been claimed by both the Viceroyalty of Peru and the Viceroyalty of New Granada (Colombia), since Ecuador was not yet a separate country. The dispute still existed at the time San Martín sailed north aboard the *Macedonia*. When he disembarked on July 25, 1822, he found Bolívar had already entered the city and was waiting to greet him. "Welcome to Colombian soil," Bolívar said, showing that he already considered Guayaquil his conquest and San Martín the outsider.

It was not an auspicious start for their meeting. In contrast to San Martín's cool aloofness, Bolívar was a slender, dynamic man of tremendous energies and almost hypnotic powers of persuasion. Where San Martín was basically a military leader, Bolívar was both soldier and politician. He had written extensively on political themes and had instituted constitutions in the countries he had freed, according to his long-range political plans. Only thirty-nine years of age, Bolívar was just reaching the peak of his power, while San Martín at forty-four was ill, exhausted from years of fighting, and declining in popularity.

The two leaders met three times in secret, meetings unattended by even their secretaries, so that there is no record of what actually took place. But from letters both wrote later, it appears that San Martín was no match for the ambitious Bolívar.

After witnessing the internal struggles of Argentina and Chile, San Martín was convinced that a republican form of government would not work in South America. Always a believer in strong central government, he favored the eventual establishment of constitutional monarchies with foreign princes imported to act as the rulers. On the other hand, Bolívar favored a great federation of independent republics and was prepared to set up constitutions for the new countries.

Both agreed to combine their armies to defeat the Spanish forces in Peru. To make this possible, San Martín offered Bolívar the top command. Bolívar immediately refused. While it appeared to be a gracious gesture, it put San Martín at a disadvantage. Bolívar did not offer to give San Martín the top command and once they were combined the armies could not continue to follow two leaders. San Martín left the last meeting with his face grave; Bolívar was smiling as though confident of success.

On the final evening the two men attended a banquet in

their honor. Bolívar unabashedly offered the first toast. "To the two greatest men in South America, General San Martín and myself."

"For the speedy termination of the war, the organization of the different republics of the continent and the health of the liberator of Colombia," San Martín replied rather stiffly, his toast revealing his decision.

The dinner over, Bolívar stayed on for the dancing. San Martín excused himself and returned to his ship. At dawn the *Macedonia* sailed back to Peru. In Bolívar, San Martín had seen a military leader capable of carrying out the final campaign. Furthermore, when that campaign was over, Bolívar was prepared to direct the political futures of the countries, a task for which San Martín had neither talent or interest. "There is not room in Peru for both Bolívar and myself. . . . Let him enter that America may triumph," San Martín wrote to O'Higgins.

At the same time that he made the decision to turn the conquest of Peru over to Bolívar, San Martín also decided to retire from public life. In Peru he found the government in chaos again. Staying just long enough to restore order, he resigned as protector of Peru in September, 1822. "I have witnessed the independence of the states of Chile and Peru; I have in my hand the standard which Pizarro brought to enslave the empire of the Incas; and I have ceased to be a public man. . . . My promises to the countries for which I have fought are fulfilled: to secure their independence and leave them to select their own governments," he said in his final statement to the people.

From Peru, San Martín sailed to Chile, where he was delayed briefly by illness, but O'Higgins' government was tottering. By the time San Martín had crossed the Andes to

Mendoza, where he stopped again to convalesce, word reached him that O'Higgins had been forced to resign and flee into exile in Peru. Then San Martín learned of the death of his wife in Buenos Aires. Argentina had no place for its former hero. In Buenos Aires, San Martín stopped just long enough to order a tombstone for his wife's grave bearing the epitaph: "Here lies Remedios Escalada San Martín, wife and friend of General San Martín." Then with his young daughter, he set sail for exile in Europe.

The remaining years of San Martín's life were spent first at Brussels, then in a modest country home outside Paris. He devoted his time to the education of his daughter until her marriage. After that he became a virtual recluse, spending his time with his correspondence and books.

For the first few years of exile, San Martín wrote hopefully to his friends of someday returning to the colonies, particularly after 1824, when Bolívar's armies achieved the final triumph over the Spaniards. But the newly freed republics did not establish the orderly governments that San Martín had envisioned. In 1840 Bolívar was overthrown, and he died on his way to exile. Two years later O'Higgins died also, still an exile in Peru. After that San Martín stopped writing of returning and seemed content to remain in Europe, where he died in 1850 at the age of seventy-two.

He was buried first in the Cathedral of Boulogne, but later his body was removed and reinterred in a place of honor in the Cathedral at Buenos Aires. Almost forgotten during his later years, he is recognized today as Argentina's greatest patriot and a hero of all South America.

5 ▨ The Great Liberator
SIMÓN BOLÍVAR, 1783–1814

For a man who was to liberate half a continent, earn the title, "The Great Liberator," and become South America's greatest hero, Simón Bolívar got off to an incredibly slow start. A spoiled child, an undisciplined youth, and finally, an arrogant, self-indulgent, young man, he was known as an international playboy by the time he was twenty-three. Yet, events had taken place during his youth that would precipitate the great change that was to redirect his life.

Simón Bolívar was born in Caracas, Venezuela, on July 24, 1783, the youngest child in an enormously wealthy Creole family whose ancestors had settled in South America in the sixteenth century. Politically, Venezuela was only a captain-generalcy; economically it was the most progressive of Spain's American colonies. Located in northeastern South America, its long coastline on the Caribbean Sea made it the most accessible of the colonies to both Spain and the islands of the Caribbean. Though it did not compete with Peru or Mexico in mineral production, the cacao, tobacco, sugar, and indigo produced on its rich plantations were vital to Spain.

At the time of Bolívar's birth, Venezuela's population of about 750,000 persons was largely concentrated along the northern coast, as it still is today. There in the hot, tropical lowlands were the great plantations, owned by wealthy Creoles and worked by Negro slaves. Rising behind these lowlands was a range of coastal mountains, low enough to permit travel into the interior, but high enough to provide a more healthful climate. Caracas, the bustling capital of about 40,000 people, was located in the foothills, but with ready access to the port of La Guaira on the humid flatlands below.

In the interior beyond these coastal mountains and stretching hundreds of miles south to the jungle forests along the Orinoco River were great grasslands similar to the Argentine *pampas*. Only here in the more humid northern regions they were called *llanos*. The few scattered cities had originated as mission settlements serving the needs of the Indians. But just as the *pampas* had produced the *gauchos*, the *llanos* were largely inhabited by tribes of mixed-breed, nomadic horsemen called *llaneros*, who followed their own local chieftains and had little interest in the city dwellers along the coast. Farther inland in the jungles of the Orinoco to the south and on the slopes of the northern Andes that separated Venezuela from Colombia, were scattered Indian tribes that had little or no contact with civilization.

The first Creole settlers went to Venezuela by way of the Caribbean Islands. They were traders by nature. From the beginning they resented the trade restrictions imposed on them by Spain. Spain had lost many of her island possessions to France, Holland, and Britain. The citizens of these Caribbean colonies and even the United States were eager to trade with Venezuela. With the Venezuelans equally eager for commerce, Spanish trade restrictions were frequently overlooked or openly flouted. When foreign vessels entered Venezuelan ports, they brought the usual influx of new ideas, which stimulated the Creoles to even more independent thought.

However, this spirit of independence existed only among the wealthy upper class. They sought economic liberation, not social reform. The original settlers from the Caribbean Islands brought slaves with them. Later, they imported thousands more to work their tropical plantations, so that slavery was more firmly entrenched in Venezuela than in any of the other mainland colonies. While the wealth of the Creole landowners increased, the lives of the slaves and the impoverished Indians and mestizos who worked for them remained the same. Venezuela had virtually no middle class except for a relatively small group of merchants and tradesmen in the coastal cities. To the great mass of black, Indian, or mestizo laborers it made little difference whether they paid allegiance to Spain or the Creoles.

The family of Simón Bolívar was one of the oldest and wealthiest in Venezuela. In addition to a town house in Caracas, they owned plantations outside the city and additional ranch property on the *llanos*. Bolívar had few memories of his father, who died when he was three, but his early years, spent mostly at the country hacienda with his frail mother and older sisters and brother, were happy. A retinue of servants and slaves catered to their needs. On Sundays Bolívar accompanied his mother as she was carried to church in a canopied litter borne by four male Negro slaves in gold-trimmed livery, while four female slaves dressed in white walked behind, carrying her parasol, gloves, prayer book, and rosary.

When Bolívar was nine his mother died of tuberculosis. The older children were sent away to school, but Bolívar was taken to Caracas to live in the home of a wealthy uncle, who had been appointed his guardian.

A spoiled, headstrong boy, Bolívar made life miserable for a succession of monks his uncle brought to the house to educate him. Finally the uncle arranged for Simón Rodríguez, a brilliant young scholar who had recently returned from Europe, to become Bolívar's tutor and companion. Rodríguez came from a respected Venezuelan family, and the uncle did not know that during his studies in Europe the young scholar had been inspired by the liberal ideas of the French writers of that time. Rodríguez's favorite writer was Jean Jacques Rousseau, who believed that every man was born innocent and pure, only to be corrupted by the institutions around him. He thought a youth brought up as a child of nature who was exposed to only the finest books could become a great leader. In young Bolívar, a youth of good family heritage, Rodríguez saw a chance to test these theories.

Once he overcame his initial rebellion against any authority, Bolívar's life with Rodríguez was happy. No longer confined to Caracas, he was able to return with Rodríguez to the family hacienda outside of the city. Here the two rode and swam together. Lessons were not taught in a classroom, but delivered as they rode side by side along a mountain trail or lay naked on the rocks, drying themselves after a swim. They visited the camps of the tough *llaneros* on the family ranches on the plains, where they ate the same fare as the others and slept on the ground, and where Bolívar perfected his horsemanship. Even the *llaneros* praised him as the finest rider they had ever seen. This delighted Bolívar. Though he was slight in build, he did not like to be bested in anything.

Bolívar liked the physical training, and some of Rodríguez's liberal ideas must have penetrated his mind. However, his tutor often despaired, for Bolívar's background as a rich aristocrat had already colored his thinking. Once, after a lecture on the equality of man, Rodríguez pointed out the difference between Bolívar's rich suit and the ragged garments of an Indian boy they had just passed. Anxious to please his teacher, Bolívar galloped back, stripped off his fine velvet garments, and handed them to the Indian. Rodríguez threw up his hands in despair. "That is charity, not democracy! For a man to be equal, he must be given the chance to work and earn his own decent clothes."

To Bolívar, who had always been rich, these ideas were hard to grasp. Independent in spirit, he was not ready to accept everything his tutor said. "You say God is all powerful. If He intended men to be equal, why didn't He make them that way Himself?" he once asked Rodríguez.

When Bolívar was fourteen, the training ended abruptly. There was an attempted liberal revolt in Caracas. Rodríguez was implicated as one of the conspirators and deported. Appalled at the education his nephew must have been receiving, Bolívar's uncle did not hire another tutor. Instead, Bolívar was enrolled in the Royal Cadet Corps, an exclusive organization composed of boys from Venezuela's oldest families.

It was an easy life. The cadets received little military education. Their primary functions were to wear fancy uniforms, act as unofficial guards at the palace of the captain-general, and dance with the ladies at important government functions. It was a life Bolívar enjoyed almost as much as his outdoor training with Rodríguez. He was sent to Europe to complete his education when he was sixteen.

In Spain, Bolívar made his home with another wealthy uncle, who traveled in court circles. Bolívar had been a member of Venezuela's aristocracy, but in Spain he discovered that Creoles were regarded as inferior to native-born Spaniards. Even the fine manners he had displayed at the captain-general's palace were considered so uncouth that he had to undergo weeks of training in dancing, fencing, and languages before his uncle would present him at court. Once he made his court appearance, Bolívar quickly became part of the crowd that surrounded the youthful Prince Ferdinand.

Bolívar's favor at court was short-lived. One day in the

course of a lively game of ball, Bolívar inadvertently knocked off Ferdinand's hat. The future king, who was even more spoiled than Bolívar, insisted on an apology. Bolívar refused. "If I ever choose to strike you on purpose, you will know it," he replied hotly. Only the intervention of the queen broke up the quarrel, but after that Bolívar's standing at court declined.

Bolívar did not mind. He had fallen in love with Maria Teresa del Toro, a young woman from a wealthy Venezuelan family residing in Spain. Both his family and hers approved of the marriage, but insisted that Bolívar wait until his eighteenth birthday. The wait was not easy for the tempestuous Bolívar.

Most South Americans living in Spain were tremendously wealthy. In order to keep them in their place as Creoles, the crown forbade them to wear excessive jewelry. One morning, while riding, Bolívar was accosted by a party of soldiers who tried to arrest him because of his diamond cufflinks. With his usual impetuousness, Bolívar unseated the Spanish officer and fled. The intervention of friends kept him from being imprisoned, but it was tactfully suggested that he go into exile in France until the incident was forgotten.

Bolívar liked life in Paris. He was particularly impressed by Napoleon, who had just risen to the office of first consul. Temporarily, Napoleon became Bolívar's idol, but he had not forgotten Maria. He sent her presents from France. Shortly after his eighteenth birthday, he returned to Spain, where they were married and then they set sail for Venezuela.

With Maria beside him, Bolívar appeared to be ready to settle down as a landowner, devoting his life to his estates. After only a few months of an idyllic honeymoon at the hacienda outside Caracas, Maria was striken with tropical fever and she died within hours. Bolívar had to be restrained from committing suicide. When he recovered from the first grief, he vowed that he would never marry again. South America seemed unbearable without Maria, and he set sail for Europe.

He stopped only briefly in Spain. The nation was suffering a famine; and Creoles were forbidden to take up residence in order to preserve food supplies for the natives. Continuing to France, Bolívar entertained lavishly, became a favorite at the salon of the famous courtesan Fanny du Villars, and affected a kind of slouch hat, which became the rage of Paris as the "Chapeau Bolívar." But despite his outward appearance as a playboy, his life was not happy. He had begun to suffer from severe depressions. "My life is a desert," he wrote to Madame Villars.

More disillusionment came when Napoleon had himself declared emperor. Bolívar's former idolization turned to hatred. Though invited to the coronation, he refused to go, remaining in his rooms behind closed curtains as the coronation procession passed. About this time Bolívar contacted his old teacher, Simón Rodríguez, who was teaching in Vienna, and the two planned a walking trip through Europe. Sleeping in the open, hiking through the Alps, then going on into Italy seemed to renew Bolívar's health and spirits. But they reached Rome just in time to see Napoleon crowned emperor of Italy also.

The events of the past and the tumult of the present seemed to reach a seething climax in Bolívar's mind. One night after dinner, he and Rodríguez climbed to the top of the Aventine Hill, where they sat looking down on the lights of Rome. Suddenly Bolívar leaped to his feet. "I swear before God, I shall not rest until I have set all of South America free from the tyranny of Spain!" he cried. At twenty-three, in a moment of enlightenment, he seemed to have found his purpose in life.

Fulfilling this promise was a different matter. For almost a year longer Bolívar dallied in Europe, but in February, 1807, he returned to South America. He was in immediate demand at all the Creole social functions, for he brought news of the latest dances, fashions, and court gossip. But his true feelings suddenly burst out one night at a dinner at the palace of the captain-general. Bolívar rose suddenly to offer a toast: "To the independence of South America."

There was stunned silence. Friends tried to cover the remark with a babble of conversation. Even the Spaniards were embarrassed. The Bolívar family was much too important for any serious action to be taken against them, but Bolívar was asked to leave Caracas and remain at his hacienda in the country. It was an ineffective punishment, for the hacienda immediately became the meeting place for the liberals.

In 1810, after news of Napoleon's invasion of Spain, reached Caracas, the citizens sent home the old captain-general and set up their own independent *junta*. The action occurred on Holy Thursday, April 19, 1810. Bolívar was still in exile in the country, but a friend galloped out to the hacienda with the news. Mounting their horses, Bolívar and his older brother rode into Caracas to offer their services. The new *junta*, like the first governments that would soon be formed in the other colonies, professed loyalty to the deposed Ferdinand VII. Remembering the petulant prince who had whimpered and cried when his hat was knocked off, Bolívar wanted no part of the weakling king, and he secretly joined a small group that advocated complete independence. The Bolívars were too wealthy and influential to be ignored. The *junta* then decided to get the dangerous Bolívar brothers out of the country by appointing them ambassadors to England and the United States.

Bolívar's instructions were to try to get financial support

from the British government and to avoid Francisco Miranda, the fiery Venezuelan expatriate who was fomenting revolutionary ideas abroad. Bolívar's first act was to go to Miranda's lodgings.

Miranda was sixty years old but still a handsome and imposing man, slightly under 6 feet tall with a muscular build, piercing gray eyes, a high forehead, and thick gray hair, which he usually wore powdered, tied into a pigtail, and tucked inside his collar. Like Bolívar, Miranda had been born in Caracas, the son of a prosperous merchant. Because his family was newly emigrated from the Canary Islands, they did not belong to the landed aristocracy. Seeing little future for himself in the colonies, Miranda went to Spain, where his father's money purchased him a commission in the army. He was an able officer, but in Spain he found himself discriminated against also because of his Creole birth. During the American Revolution he fought with the Spanish forces that helped the United States drive the British out of Florida. A few years later, when he was falsely accused of profiteering, he fled the Spanish army with a price on his head and sought refuge in the United States.

Miranda had already read many of the works of the revolutionary writers of that day, and in the United States he became even more determined that his native Venezuela should be freed. Returning to Europe, he toured the countries outside of Spain, trying to stir up support for a South American rebellion without success.

Later he fought as a general in the French Revolution, then moved to England, where his home became the headquarters for the Lautaro Lodge. During 1805 and 1806, he returned to the United States, where with private funds he outfitted a small expedition that attempted an unsuccessful landing in Venezuela. Repulsed by both the Spanish army

FRANCISCO MIRANDA

and the Venezuelan people, who were not yet ready for revolution, he returned to England to take up his political activities again.

In Francisco Miranda with his flamboyant background, Bolívar found a new idol to replace the fallen Napoleon. Soon Miranda and the handsome Bolívar were seen everywhere together—at the races, parties, and balls. Bolívar's original mission was a failure. England and Spain had patched up their centuries of differences to unite against Napoleon. Bolívar could not secure money from England; but he returned to Venezuela with Miranda's promise to follow and to help with the liberation of the colony.

In Caracas, the *junta* was dismayed at Bolívar's actions. They had expected him to return with his pockets jangling with English pounds. Instead, he was bringing an aging patriot who was known around the world for the unrest he had caused. But when Miranda disembarked in December, 1810, dressed in the uniform of a French general, with all his medals blazing, a two-cornered blue hat on his powdered hair, and a single gold earring in his ear, the crowds led by Bolívar and his friends burst into frenzied cheers. After this public reception, the *junta* somewhat begrudgingly accepted the new arrival. Seizing on his military experience, they named Miranda head of the Venezuelan army.

It was not the *junta* but Bolívar who was next to become disenchanted with Miranda. After years of service with the well-outfitted, well-disciplined armies of Europe, Miranda was appalled by the ragtag collection of soldiers that Venezuela called its army. The majority of the officers were equally ill trained. Their only experience had been gained as members of the Royal Cadets.

"You call yourself a colonel," he scoffed one evening while attending a dinner given by Bolívar. "I fought dozens of battles before I attained such a rank. You have fought none."

As Miranda's host, Bolívar controlled his temper, but the remark was not forgotten. Another of his idols was beginning to topple. A short time later, when Miranda publicly upbraided Bolívar for showing off his horsemanship in front of the troops, the rift widened. However, they were still devoted to the same cause, meeting secretly with other Creoles who desired complete separation from Spain. Gradually this liberal element gained power in the government and on July 5, 1811, Venezuela declared her independence and raised the new red, yellow, and blue flag of the First Republic. The flag was patterned after the one Miranda had carried earlier in his ill-fated expedition of 1806: red for the blood shed by the patriots; blue for the high purpose of their cause; and yellow for the sands of South America.

The Spaniards still held much of Venezuela. The new army had to go into action almost immediately against the city of Valencia. Such hostility had grown between Miranda and Bolívar that Miranda refused to let Bolívar lead a regiment on the grounds that his inexperience and insubordination might endanger them all. Bolívar found a way to ignore the orders by taking a position as aide to the Marquis del Toro, a relative of his deceased wife, and riding into battle with the others.

The Spaniards had fortified themselves in a monastery inside the city. When the Marquis was wounded in the attack, Bolívar assumed command, leading charge after charge on the monastery walls. It finally took a siege to bring the city to surrender, but Bolívar had acquitted himself with such courage in his first battle that even Miranda had to cite him for valor.

The new government, beset by a thousand problems, teetered along precariously until March 16, 1812, when Venezuela was hit by one of the worst earthquakes in its history. The date was Holy Thursday, the anniversary of the founding of the first independent *junta*, two years earlier. Thousands of people were trapped in the collapsing churches, where they had gathered in observance of the holiday. An estimated 12,000 were killed.

Bolívar was in his townhouse when the tremors began. Though most of his house was demolished, he ran into the street, where he began directing operations to save those trapped in the rubble. Bursting into one city square, he found hundreds of survivors kneeling in prayer, while a monk whipped them into hysterical fear by telling them the earthquake was God's punishment for deserting King Ferdinand. Furious because these people were needed to help save the victims trapped in the wreckage, Bolívar ordered the monk seized by some passing soldiers. Then he leaped onto the building block on which the monk had been standing. "If nature has joined forces with tyranny, then I say let us fight nature, too," he cried.

Only a few of those kneeling in the square responded. The rest were too dazed to act. The situation grew steadily worse. The clergy, who had never supported the republic, continued to rouse the superstitious people into religious frenzy, insisting the earthquake was God's punishment. As additional proof, they pointed out that the areas of Venezuela still under Spanish control had suffered almost no damage. At Coro, a Spanish naval officer, Domingo Monteverde, took advantage of the situation to lead the Spanish forces in Venezuela in a new attack on the republican cities. In vain the *junta* tried to rally the people; public opinion was turning against them. Finally in desperation they gave Miranda dictatorial powers as head of both the government and the army to try to save the country.

Perhaps Miranda realized that Bolívar was the one man in Venezuela who posed a threat to his own power. Perhaps he did not trust Bolívar's impetuousness and lack of discipline. Instead of allowing Bolívar to march north with the main force of the army against Monteverde, Miranda assigned him to the seemingly minor duty of guarding the port city of Puerto Cabello, where a huge fortress housed a number of Spanish prisoners along with the main arsenal for the Venezuelan army.

The assignment was the final blow to Bolívar's pride. On his arrival at Puerto Cabello, he gave one of his lesser officers the duty of changing guards at the fortress and set up his own headquarters in the local city hall. At first, he received news of Miranda's success in taking the town of La Victoria, but there Miranda's forces seemed to bog down. Instead of pursuing his advantage and pushing on against Monteverde, Miranda set up new headquarters and began bickering with his officers over the next move. In Puerto Cabello, Bolívar was furious. Right or wrong, he never hesitated about anything.

On a June morning in 1812, Bolívar's worries about Miranda's inadequacy were interrupted by distant gunfire, then the roar of a cannonade. While Bolívar idled in the city hall, his own officers had mutinied and released the Spanish prisoners at the fortress. In dismay and fury, Bolívar rounded up a force of 250 soldiers and townsmen and led a charge on the fortress. Only 7 escaped death or injury. When an appeal to Miranda to send help went unanswered, Bolívar escaped by sea with a handful of officers.

On the voyage to La Guaira, the port city of Caracas, Bolívar's companions thought he had gone mad. White-faced, he paced the deck and talked to himself, as though he could not believe he could have been responsible for such a catastrophe. The disaster had only begun. On July 25, at the insistence of many of the wealthy Creoles, Miranda signed an armistice with Monteverde. As part of the agreement, it was rumored, he was to be given a sum of money and allowed to flee the country. The anger Bolívar had turned against himself found a new outlet against Miranda, who he felt had betrayed the country.

Bolívar was not alone in this opinion. On the night of July 30, learning that Miranda was sleeping at the home of the port commander of La Guaira in preparation for sailing the next morning, Bolívar and a number of other Creole officers secretly entered the house. While Miranda slept in an adjoining room, they held a trial. Bolívar favored executing Miranda for treason, but was overruled. Instead they went into Miranda's room, made him a prisoner, and turned him over to Spanish authorities at the port.

Miranda was imprisoned briefly in Venezuela, taken later to Puerto Rico, and finally returned to Spain, where he was held in a prison outside Cádiz until his death in 1816. Asked by a fellow prisoner if he did not find his chains heavy, Miranda replied, "Not so heavy as the ones they put on me that night at La Guaira."

Following Miranda's brief trial and betrayal to the Spaniards, Bolívar joined hundreds of other refugees who were trying to flee Caracas before Monteverde arrived. The ships in the harbor were already filled with refugees. For several weeks he hid in the home of royalist friends. Finally his friends received permission for him to leave Caracas unmolested on the grounds that he had done Spain a service by capturing Miranda. For the first time in his life, Bolívar found himself without friends, his name clouded for having betrayed Miranda. But he was developing into a determined leader. All over South America the other colonies were also asserting their independence, and Bolívar set sail for Cartagena, Colombia.

While Venezuela had been only a captain-generalcy, Colombia was part of the Viceroyalty of New Granada, which also included Panama and most of Ecuador. The colony was so large that there had been no unified movement for independence. Several major cities had set up their own independent *juntas* and were fighting the Spaniards and quarreling among themselves.

The government at Cartagena welcomed Bolívar, but the commander of their army was distrustful. He assigned Bolívar to the remote garrison of Barranca on the Magdalena River, with orders to guard the town and make no other move. Bolívar's command consisted of 200 Negro soldiers, most of them without uniforms and armed only with wooden lances, but Bolívar started drilling them immediately and recruited more Negro warriors from the tropical jungles around the town.

Typically, he ignored his orders. When his men were ready, he loaded them into dugout canoes called *bongos* and started up the river, capturing town after town in surprise night attacks. His commander furiously ordered him back to face court martial, but Bolívar went over his head to the government. Delighted with his successes, they told Bolívar to go on. As he moved farther into the interior, Bolívar was joined by additional units of Colombian soldiers from other independent cities in the interior.

By February 13, 1813, they had reached the city of Cúcuta near the Venezuelan border. The town was well defended. After four hours of fighting, Bolívar's men were running out of ammunition, and they were no closer to victory than they had been in the beginning. One of Bolívar's greatest talents

SIMÓN BOLÍVAR

as commander was his audacity in attempting what the opposition least expected. When his officers pointed out that their ammunition was almost gone and suggested a retreat, Bolívar issued exactly the opposite orders, sending his men against the enemy in a bayonet charge as though they had already won the position and had reinforcements right behind them. Taken by surprise, the Spaniards fell back and abandoned the city.

The fall of Cúcuta brought freedom to most of Colombia. Following the victory, Bolívar addressed his soldiers from horseback. "In two months you have completed two campaigns and begun a third, which starts here today and will end in the land of my birth."

With a victorious army under his command, Bolívar was determined to move on across the border to free Venezuela. There were protests from many of the Colombian soldiers, who had no desire to fight on foreign soil. Bolívar ignored the grumbling and called a meeting of his officers, at which he gave them orders to march.

Chagrin showed on many of the officers' faces. Only one young lieutenant, Francisco Santander, who had just celebrated his twenty-first birthday, had the courage to speak. "I will not lead Colombian soldiers onto Venezuelan soil," he protested.

Enraged at such an affront, Bolívar whirled on the young upstart. Drawing a pistol, he laid it on a table. "You will march or one of two things will happen. Either you will have to shoot me, or what is more likely, I shall pick up that gun and shoot you," he said coldly.

While the other officers held their breath, the two men stared at each other. Santander, a studious, grave-faced youth, had been trained for the law, not the army. His eyes were the first to waver. Stepping back in place, he agreed to march.

Bolívar was rarely generous toward those who opposed him, but perversely he seemed stirred to admiration of the young lieutenant's spunk. To everyone's surprise, Bolívar ignored the incident and soon elevated Santander to the rank of colonel, and Santander became one of his most trusted officers.

Bolívar moved across the border, encountering only minor opposition at first. Everywhere he found tragedy and desolation. In the treaty signed with Miranda, Monteverde had promised no reprisals. He had not kept his word. His soldiers had left a trail of death and butchery. The entire population of some villages, including women and children, had been purposely maimed as punishment for aiding the patriots. One Spanish general carried a bagful of human ears, which he awarded to his soldiers in place of medals. At first Bolívar was sickened by the butchery; then he became hardened to it and some of his men became equally brutal.

With each battle Bolívar was learning valuable lessons in military strategy. Monteverde threw his forces at Bolívar in the form of a triangle, a classic maneuver in which the enemy is permitted to break through one side of the formation and is then trapped between the other two sides. Warned by his scouts, Bolívar divided his army and struck two sides of the triangle at once, so that Monteverde was trapped. When Bolivar's infantry was unable to march fast enough to launch a surprise attack, he mounted one foot soldier behind each cavalryman and sent them off under the cover of darkness. At dawn, Monteverde found that a regiment of both infantry and cavalry had miraculously sprung up behind him overnight.

Then a frantic message reached Bolívar, stating that after he had taken the army into Venezuela the Spaniards had surged back and were recapturing Colombian cities. Bolívar replied that he was too close to victory in Venezuela to waste his

FRANCISCO SANTANDER

army by turning back. This was true. Monteverde and his forces withdrew to Puerto Cabello, and early in August, 1813, Bolívar entered Caracas unopposed.

"The Liberator! The Liberator!" the crowds cheered as they lined the streets. They were equal to the crowds Bolívar

had seen welcoming Napoleon in Paris. Bolívar delighted in
the plaudits of the crowd, but he was resolved he would never
make himself an emperor as Napoleon had done. It was a
difficult promise to keep. The government was bankrupt and
the Spaniards still controlled many towns. The Second Republic of Venezuela was founded with Bolívar as dictator
until the country could be pacified. "When the war is over, I
shall give up all my powers and see that a republican government is established," he promised.

It was a precarious government. Monteverde still held
Puerto Cabello. To supply his army, Bolívar levied taxes that
were unpopular. In eastern Venezuela, republican forces led
by two other Venezuelan leaders, Santiago Marino and
Manuel Piar, had set up a separate Venezuelan government
of their own. Bolívar tried unsuccessfully to get Marino and
Piar to join his government.

There was more trouble when an army of the fierce *llaneros*,
led by their own leader, Thomás Boves, joined Monteverde.
The *llaneros* were wild, unpredictable, and fierce fighters.
Bolívar turned back one attack, but Boves soon organized another army. So many Spanish soldiers had been taken prisoner
that the possibility of mutiny had also become a threat. Bolívar gave orders that all, even those in the hospitals, were to
be executed. The order brought horrified protests from around
the world.

Nothing could stem the tide that was turning against him.
With Boves' army moving in from one side and Monteverde's from the other, Bolívar sent a frantic plea to Marino
for support. When it failed to come, he was forced to evacuate
Caracas. All over the city the church bells began to ring the
alarm, while soldiers ran from house to house telling the
people to pack what they could carry and get out of the city.
The people left the city by the thousands, fleeing toward

Barcelona, 250 miles to the east. Hundreds dropped from exhaustion or died of starvation along the way. Those who fell behind were slaughtered by Boves' pursuing troops. Entire families committed suicide. Fathers threw their children from cliffs along the road, preferring to see them die instantly on the rocks below than maimed and tortured by Boves. Exhausted mothers stood by the trail weeping and holding up infants, begging the mounted soldiers to take them on their horses. Many of the soldiers were unable to resist the pleas and rode carrying babies in their arms with other children hanging on behind them. Six thousand people perished along the trail to Barcelona.

Bolívar rode alone, his face rigidly set as though he did not see the suffering. His days as an emotional youth were past. He could no longer allow himself to be compassionate. Only the Cause mattered. The Cause must prevail.

There was no safety in Barcelona either. The survivors had to go on to Cumaná. Too late, Marino and Piar brought up their forces. They could not stop Boves either. At Cumaná, Bolívar loaded all the gold and valuables he could salvage aboard a ship and fled the country with Marino, Piar, and forty other officers.

Once Bolívar had condemned Miranda for doing this same thing. Now he realized the truth: a dead leader cannot save a country. Only by fleeing with all the wealth he could gather could he return to launch another campaign of liberation.

In September, 1814, Bolívar reached Cartagena, Colombia. They were fighting the Spanish soldiers, too, and the country was torn with dissension. By spring of 1815, seeing that Colombia seemed further split by his presence, Bolívar reluctantly set sail for exile in Jamaica to begin the darkest period of his life.

6 ❋ The Final Victory
SIMÓN BOLÍVAR, 1815–1830

Two attempts to set up a Venezuelan republic had failed. Between the earthquake and the war, one quarter of the population of Venezuela had lost their lives in a six-year period. In Spain, Ferdinand VII had been restored to the throne and was preparing to send 10,000 soldiers under the able General Pablo Morillo to wipe out the last pockets of rebellion in the colonies.

Though Bolívar was only thirty-two years old when he stepped ashore at Jamaica, he looked years older. His dark hair was already streaked with white. He was racked with the hacking cough of the early stages of tuberculosis. His hollow cheeks accentuated his thin, hawklike nose; his dark eyes were sunken and feverish. "The flames have absorbed all of the oil," the Jamaican governor commented, shocked at his altered appearance.

In spite of his changed appearance and the defeats he had suffered, Bolívar had no intention of giving up. In Jamaica, surrounded by books and papers, he began working out a new plan for liberation, not only of Venezuela but of all South America, making out detailed outlines on the kind of government to be set up in each country. He envisioned a great federation of South American states with headquarters at Panama. He suggested building a canal across the Isthmus to promote world trade. Because he did not believe that the South American people were ready for self-government, he proposed that a president to be elected for life should head each country. His favorite project was the establishment of a new country to be named Gran Colombia, created out of a combination of Venezuela, Colombia, and Ecuador.

These plans, published later under the name of the *Jamaica Letters*, would establish Bolívar's fame as a writer and political thinker as well as a military man. But in 1815, most of the world considered him mad.

Spain considered Bolívar a dangerous madman. One evening, when Bolívar was visiting a woman friend, an old comrade from Colombia called at his lodgings. As the hour grew late and Bolívar did not return, the friend made himself comfortable in Bolívar's hammock. In the morning Bolívar found the man dead, killed during the night by Spanish assassins, who had mistaken the Colombian for Bolívar in the darkness.

Shortly after this assassination attempt Bolívar fled again, this time to Haiti. More than twenty years had passed since Toussaint L'Ouverture had led his slave armies to victory. Northern Haiti was still under the dictatorial rule of one of L'Ouverture's lieutenants, but in the south a mild-mannered but brilliant mulatto, Alexandre Pétion, was president of the Republic of Haiti, the only republic still surviving in the New World outside of the United States. Though Haiti was a small country with problems of her own, Pétion offered Bolívar sanctuary and whatever help he could give. In return Bolívar promised that his first act on landing on South American soil would be the emancipation of all the slaves.

From various islands of the Caribbean, other exiled patriots went to Haiti to join Bolívar. The 10,000 Spanish soldiers led by General Pablo Morillo had reoccupied both Venezuela and Colombia. But deep in the interior there were areas of resistance. Santander, the young Colombian officer who had once defied Bolívar, had not fled into the exile with the others.

With part of the Colombian army he was hiding out in the mountains along the Colombian border. Tomás Boves, the *llanero* who had fought so fiercely against Bolívar, had been killed in the final days of battle. On the plains the *llaneros* were following a new leader, José Páez, and they were fighting against the Spaniards. Bolívar hoped to land on the coast and somehow unite all these forces. "We are leaving with fourteen ships, two thousand men and enough ammunition to last ten years. Tell all your friends," he wrote to a relative.

It was a gross lie. When the expedition got under way, there were 250 men and seven small ships with only one cannon, but Bolívar knew the power of propaganda. This time, unfortunately, it did not work. Marino and Piar got a foothold along the eastern coast near Cumaná and Barcelona, but Bolívar, who attempted a landing near Caracas, was defeated and forced back to Haiti.

Undaunted, he began to plan the next move. Friends in England secured unexpected assistance. In Europe, the defeat of Napoleon had released thousands of soldiers. Spanish soldiers were sent to South America, but hundreds of British and Irish soldiers, unable to find jobs at home, were recruited to fight for Bolívar. On New Year's Day, 1817, Bolívar set sail for Venezuela again. This time he did not attempt a direct attack on Caracas. After contacting Marino and Piar at Barcelona, his ships sailed farther east to the mouth of the great Orinoco River, then 200 miles up the river, where they seized the jungle town of Angostura (called Ciudad Bolívar today). There, where his forces could be supplied by boats coming up the river and he could contact the other leaders in the interior, Bolívar set up his new capital.

As always, the new government had problems, one being the jealousy of Bolívar's other generals. When Marino once again tried to set up his own government, Bolívar traveled to the coast to see him. After he was gone, Piar attempted to take over the government at Angostura. On his return, Bolívar ordered Piar arrested, although he was one of Bolívar's ablest generals. No one believed any harm would come to him, but Bolívar had already proved he could be ruthless when he ordered the execution of the Spanish prisoners. Equally ruthless now, he ordered Piar executed. After that, he had less trouble with insubordination.

Bitter experience had taught Bolívar the folly of attacking the coastal cities of Venezuela. His new plan was to move on them from the *llanos* in the interior but it hinged on getting the support of the *llaneros*. Under Boves they had fought against Bolívar. Now they seemed to be fighting as fiercely against the Spaniards, but Bolívar knew they were unpredictable. If they did not like his appearance as a leader, they could turn against him just as quickly.

It took Bolívar and his men a month to travel 400 miles up the Orinoco, then follow its tributary, the Apure, northwest onto the plains. Along the way their uniforms and shoes wore out and they were reduced to eating the turtle eggs they dug from the sand along the river. But when they reached the agreed meeting place, Páez and 2,000 men were waiting.

On horseback, Páez was an imposing figure with his broad muscular shoulders and thick, curly chestnut hair and beard. It was only when he dismounted that he revealed himself as a rather small man with thin, spindly legs out of proportion to his powerful chest and head. His men were an equally strange-looking army, sitting astride their horses, barebacked and barefooted, wearing short breeches sewn from animal hides, bright kerchiefs tied around their heads, and armed only with long hardwood spears. Bolívar knew they were among the best horsemen in all South America. For several moments Bolívar and Páez appraised each other warily; then some spark of brotherhood seemed to ignite between them and they embraced while the men of both sides burst into cheers.

At twenty-nine, Páez was seven years younger than Bolívar. The son of a poor mestizo farmer who worked a small hard-scrabble farm on the edge of the plains, he had run away to the *llanos* when he was seventeen, after killing a man in a fight. Years of working as a cowboy had hardened him into a tough, cunning fighter. He had joined a *llanero* regiment formed by the Spaniards when he was twenty and later fought as an officer under Boves. After General Morillo's European-trained soldiers had occupied Venezuela, they had made the mistake of scoffing at the ragged *llanero* fighters. Their pride wounded, the *llaneros* had returned to the plains, reorganized under Páez, and turned to fighting the Spaniards.

In spite of the differences in their backgrounds, Páez was as daring and resourceful a fighter as Bolívar. One of his favorite tricks was to lure the Spanish soldiers out on the tinder-dry *llanos* in the hot summer season, then set prairie fires to be carried toward them. He tied cattle hides to the tails of half-wild horses and stampeded them through the enemy camps.

Those following days Páez and Bolívar were constantly to-gether. Páez seemed fascinated by Bolívar's fastidious man-ners. Though Bolívar rode like a *llanero*, slept in a hammock, and ate the same food as the common soldiers, he carried a portable bathtub with him and brushed his teeth regularly, two niceties that astounded the rough *llanero*.

Learning that Páez and Bolívar had united on the plains, Santander brought his Colombian soldiers down from the

ANTONIO PÁEZ

mountains to join them. Together they started east against the Spaniards. Their first obstacle was to cross the heavily guarded Apure River. Páez had promised that he would provide boats for the crossing. When they reached the river, Bolívar turned to him angrily. "Where are the boats you promised?" he demanded.

"There they are." Páez pointed to several heavily guarded Spanish gunboats anchored in midstream. Followed by 50 horsemen holding their lances in their teeth, he whipped his horse into the water. The Spaniards opened fire, but the *llaneros* continued, scrambled over the sides of the boats, killed the Spanish guards, and returned, towing the gunboats behind them.

Surging on, the rebel army captured the city of Calabozo; but General Morillo, who had distinguished himself fighting in Europe, was a more formidable enemy than any Bolívar had met before. Soon the Spaniards were forcing his men back onto the plains.

One evening as they made camp, Bolívar asked Santander to take command while he retired to his hammock in a grove of trees. The Spaniards had chosen that night for a daring attempt on Bolívar's life. Obtaining the password from a captured prisoner, a Spanish officer and several men disguised in rebel uniforms slipped past the outer guards, getting as far as Santander on the pretense that they carried a message for Bolívar.

For a moment, even Santander was deceived. "General, a messenger is——" he began in a normal tone of voice; then in response to some inner warning his voice ended in a cry of alarm. Half-a-dozen shots rang out, each hitting the hammock, but warned by Santander's voice, Bolívar had thrown himself safely to the ground.

The army continued its retreat to San Fernando de Apure, the *llanero* capital. After being delayed several weeks by illness, Bolívar left Páez to continue harassing Morillo from the plains while he returned to Angostura. His first campaign had come to nothing, but he had united his forces and learned the measure of his enemy.

Although he held only a small corner of Venezuelan soil, Bolívar ordered a general election. On February 15, 1819, the Third Republic of Venezuela was formed at Angostura, with Bolívar elected president and the noted Venezuelan scholar, Francisco Zea, as vice-president.

The troops being recruited abroad were beginning to reach Angostura. In March, Bolívar started back to rejoin Páez, accompanied by 500 eager British soldiers in their fine red uniforms. The 400 mile journey was as devastating as before. By the time the men reached the *llanos*, the red uniforms and shiny black boots had rotted away in the humid climate, and many of the soldiers were barefooted and dressed only in loincloths.

Bad news waited at Páez's camp. Morillo's forces had recaptured San Fernando de Apure, and Páez's men were little more than fugitives hiding out on the plains. Together, Páez and Bolívar drilled and prepared their men, but each time they tried to force an encounter, Morillo refused to allow them a decisive battle. Some of their soldiers began to desert. "Sun . . . tough meat . . . foul water. I would desert myself if I had any place to go," Bolívar remarked bitterly to Páez one night as they sat beside a campfire.

Their trials had only begun. By May the long, hot summer was over and the winter rainy season was turning the *llanos* into a vast muddy lake. Morillo withdrew his forces from San Fernando de Apure, but only to avoid the rains that made fighting almost impossible. While the Spanish forces waited out the winter in the comfort of the coastal cities, Bolívar faced the dismal prospect of months on the soggy plains, with hunger, desertion, and illness depleting his forces.

Bolívar called a meeting of his generals at a jungle hut, where he announced a daring plan. Leaving Páez in Venezuela to cover their movements, he would lead the main body of the army over the Andes to attack the Spanish forces in Colombia. The plan was so outrageous that the others were stunned. Suddenly a young Irish colonel leaped to his feet, swearing to follow Bolívar all the way to Cape Horn if necessary. His enthusiasm inspired the others and all agreed to the plan.

Taking some of the *llaneros* with his own forces, Bolívar marched west toward the mountains. Day after day his men sloshed through water up to their waists, sleeping at night on hummocks of dry ground. Following them were the army of wives and children that invariably accompanied the native troops. Finally they reached a small village at the foot of the mountains, where Santander and his men were waiting for them. For the first time in weeks they could dry out their clothes. But Santander had bad news. Two of the passes across the mountains were heavily guarded. Only La Pisba, so high it was considered impassable, was unwatched.

Undaunted, Bolívar chose La Pisba. "Where a goat can go, an army can go," he said. After allowing only four days of rest, he ordered his 3,000 men on into the mountains. San Martín, of Argentina, had planned two years for his crossing of the Andes. Bolívar's crossing was a spur-of-the-moment decision. The pass at La Pisba was only 10,000 feet high, but Bolívar was crossing it in winter. Within a few weeks all the animals had died of exhaustion or fallen from the icy trails. Soon men were dying also. The narrow trail they followed in single file was stained red with blood from their lacerated bare feet. Behind them was the equally ragged little army of scarecrow women and children.

It was mid-July before they stumbled down the other side into the Colombian village of Socha. The townspeople greeted them like heroes, giving them food and clothing, and scouring the countryside for horses. Once again Bolívar allowed only a four-day rest so that the element of surprise would not be lost. When they started again, almost the entire male population of Socha, armed with knives, pitchforks, and anything they could find, had fallen in behind them.

The Spanish forces at the town of Tunja had learned of their arrival and moved out to meet them at a river crossing. Bolívar ordered the construction of rafts to carry his British soldiers in an attack on one side of the hill, while Santander led his Colombians against the other side. After eight hours of fighting, they still had not taken the hill. Bolívar summoned the Negro commander of his company of *llaneros.* "Colonel, save your country!" he ordered.

The *llaneros* splashed through the swamp and up the hill straight into the face of the cannon. At the same time the British and Colombian soldiers surged forward in a final charge and the hill was taken. A few days later the citizens of Tunja gave Bolívar a hero's welcome. More important, they raised a thousand men to take the places of those who had fallen in the fight at the river.

On August 7, 1819, Bolívar moved out of the city, intercepting the main body of the Spanish forces at a river crossing on their way to Boyacá. Before the Spaniards could unlimber their artillery, Bolívar ordered a combined charge of both his cavalry and infantrymen. The battle was short and violent with only 50 Spanish soldiers escaping death or capture. The Battle of Boyacá ended Spanish rule in Colombia.

Bolívar started back to Angostura, leaving Santander in charge of the government of Colombia. As he made his way down the Orinoco River by canoe, he spotted another canoe coming upstream. "Who goes there," Bolívar demanded.

"General Sucre," one of the boatmen replied.

Bolívar's face turned livid. "There is no such general!" he cried and ordered both boats ashore. To his surprise he found himself looking at a sturdy young officer who was still in his early twenties, about his own height with slightly curling brown hair and an appealing boyish face with serious gray eyes.

With dignity but no sign of quailing before Bolívar's anger, the young officer replied that he had just been promoted to the rank of general by Francisco Zea, Bolívar's vice-president, but he would immediately give up the title if it did not please Bolívar. Something about the youth's dignity in contrast to his own blustering anger put Bolívar at a disadvantage. It did not seem like an auspicious meeting, but it was the beginning of the closest friendship of Bolívar's life.

Like Bolívar, Antonio de Sucre came from an old and wealthy Creole family. Born at Cumaná, he had seen most of his early service under General Marino. Unlike the majority of Bolívar's generals, who were known for their flamboyance and bluster, Sucre was quiet, reserved, and content to rise steadily in the ranks through his brilliance as an engineer and tactician. At only twenty-four, he had been elevated to general, the youngest in the army. Bolívar allowed him to keep the position and watched him closely during the following months. Of Bolívar's officers, Sucre seemed to be the only one who was completely without personal ambition. In spite of the faithful service of both Santander and Páez, Bolívar suspected that deep in his heart each gave his first allegiance to his own homeland, Colombia or Venezuela. In

ANTONIO DE SUCRE

young Sucre he saw an officer committed to the liberation of all South America, who might be groomed to someday become his successor. "If God should give to men the right to select the members of their own family, I should select for a son, General Sucre," Bolívar told his secretary.

Back in Angostura, Bolívar took the first step he had outlined years before in his *Jamaica Letters*. He dissolved the government of the Third Venezuelan Republic and announced the formation of the country of Gran Colombia, made up of Venezuela, Colombia, and Ecuador, with its temporary capital at Cúcuta, near the Colombian border. It was a government mostly on paper. Only Colombia had been freed. Venezuela and Ecuador remained in the hands of the Spaniards.

Bolívar put Sucre to his first test when he sent him as an emissary to General Morillo to arrange a temporary armistice between the enemy forces. Morillo agreed not only to the armistice but to a meeting with Bolívar. The meeting did not produce any immediate results, but its effect was far-reaching. In Spain, soldiers awaiting shipment overseas had launched a revolution at Cádiz and forced a more liberal government on Ferdinand VII. When he received this news and had his discussion with Bolívar, General Morillo decided to use the period of armistice to return to Spain to persuade Ferdinand to give up the war in the colonies. Behind him, in command of the Spanish forces, he left a much inferior general.

Bolívar took advantage of the armistice to resupply his fighting men. In the spring of 1821, he sent Sucre with 700 soldiers to begin the conquest of Ecuador, while he and Páez, using several border incidents as excuses to break the armistice, marched toward Caracas.

The new general lacked Morillo's cunning. When he met Bolívar on the plains of Carabobo on June 24, 1821, he had the Spanish guns set up to command the approaches on three sides of the valley, ignoring a supposedly impenetrable forest on the fourth side. Bolívar ordered the first attack through the forest. It took Páez three hours to hack a trail barely wide enough to admit his men in single file through the trees, but the attack caught the Spaniards by surprise. The patriot losses were heavy, but the Spanish losses were greater and with the Battle of Carabobo, Venezuela won her freedom from Spain.

Once again a victorious Bolívar rode into Caracas. Seven years had passed since he had seen his native city. There was no great rejoicing. The citizens of Caracas had paid too great a price for freedom. Many of the buildings destroyed by the great earthquake of 1812 had not yet been rebuilt; two thirds of the population had been killed. The survivors lined the streets, sullen and apathetic.

After arranging for the government of the city, Bolívar stopped at the ruins of his family hacienda on his way back to Cúcuta. Remembering the happy hours he had spent there as a boy and later with his young bride Maria, he, too, was striken with despair.

To the south, Argentina and Chile were free and, according to the latest reports, San Martín's troops were camped on the outskirts of Lima, Peru. Only Ecuador and Peru remained to be liberated. For a moment Bolívar was tempted to send word to San Martín, Sucre, and Santander to continue without him. Then the depression passed. His ambitions had extended beyond the mere liberation of South America to the kind of governments that must be set up in each country. He knew nothing of San Martín's political ambitions, only that he was a brilliant military leader. He did not trust any of them, even Sucre, to carry out his plans for South America. He alone was the one man who could control, direct, and lead them all. As ruthless with himself as he was with others, he pushed old memories aside, mounted his horse, and left the hacienda forever.

A constitution was completed for the new country of Gran Colombia with Bogotá selected as the permanent capital. Bolívar was elected president; Santander, vice-president. Páez was sent to head the government of Venezuela. The youthful Sucre had lived up to all of Bolívar's expectations. He had captured Ecuador's port city of Guayaquil, moved on into the mountains to take Riobamba, and was marching on Quito. Waiting just long enough to be sworn into office, Bolívar left Santander to govern Gran Colombia and headed south to help Sucre.

Quito was considered impregnable by its Spanish defenders because of its location high in the mountains, where their cannon controlled the approach from below. Before Bolívar could bring up his reinforcements, he learned that the city had fallen. Sucre had sent his soldiers scrambling up the slopes like mountain goats, straining and pulling their cannon with them, to attack from the heights above the city, where his men could send their cannon fire and avalanches of rocks down on the Spanish soldiers at will.

Sucre prepared a great celebration for Bolívar's arrival. Garlands of green formed arches over the streets, and three Indians carrying a 20-foot-long bamboo trumpet announced Bolívar's triumphant entry with a bleat that could be heard for miles.

Following the parade, all the Creole families of Quito turned out for a great ball in honor of the liberator. Attending the ball was Manuela Sáenz Thorne, a beautiful and controversial young woman who was separated from her English husband. She had attracted Bolívar's eye earlier, along the line of march. That evening, he made her his partner for every dance, ignoring the wives of the high officials. Bolívar had kept his vow never to remarry, but he had known many mis-tresses. In Quito, Manuela became his new mistress and con-stant companion for the rest of his life. Accompanied by Bolívar's two great mastiffs and his personal bodyguard, she went from house to house, raising money for his cause. Hav-ing only recently left Peru, she was able to tell him a great deal about his southern rival, San Martín. By this time San Martín had taken Lima, but he had been unable to proceed any farther against the Spanish forces.

Both Bolívar and San Martín sought military liberation of all South America, but Bolívar's ambitions extended even further to the governments that must be set up in the new countries. A meeting was arranged for the two leaders at Guayaquil in July, 1822. When San Martín sailed back to Lima, a few days later, it was with the understanding that he planned to withdraw from public life, leaving the final con-quest of Peru to Bolívar.

For more than a year problem after problem delayed the start of Bolívar's Peruvian campaign. An uprising in southern Colombia had to be put down. He became ill and spent many weeks recovering. Word came from Gran Colombia that, just as he had feared, Santander and Páez were quarreling over the rights of each of their countries.

It was September, 1823, before Bolívar finally reached Cal-lao, the port city of Lima. Even then, the ever-faithful Sucre had gone ahead of him to prepare the way. Soon after reach-ing Lima, Bolívar realized why San Martín had run into dif-ficulty. Peru was a morass of corruption and intrigue.

Within a short time, Bolívar had to sail north to put down a rebellion at the town of Trujillo. On his way back to Lima he became desperately ill. Believing that he was dying, his

San Martín and Bolívar at Guayaquil, Ecuador

men took him ashore to a small fishing village. By the time he had begun to recover, the Spaniards had retaken Lima in his absence.

"Your Excellency, what will you do now?" a friend asked.

Lying flat on his back, Bolívar looked up at him with burning eyes. "Triumph!" he roared.

Returning to Trujillo, Bolívar outfitted still another army. He was joined by Manuela, who had escaped Lima on muleback, with all of his government papers, by crossing an arm of the Andes that separated Trujillo from southern Peru. Since he lacked ships to carry his army to Callao by sea, Bolívar planned to return to Peru by this same route, crossing the Andes again. This time he did not launch his threadbare troops over the mountains unprepared, but made plans as detailed those of San Martín.

Women sewed heavy green uniforms to protect the men in the high altitudes. Indians were sent ahead to scout out trails, build wooden shelters, and hide caches of supplies along the way. In June, 1824, Bolívar started across the mountains with 9,000 men. They followed a number of trails, communicating with each other by means of huge trumpets that echoed and reechoed from the mountain peaks. On August 6, 1824, they met the enemy on the plain of Junín, so high in the mountains that the men could not bear the exertion of fighting in the high altitudes for more than an hour. Bolívar's forces won the battle, but the main body of the Spanish army escaped.

Before Bolívar could pursue them, orders from Gran Colombia forbade him to lead the army into battle again for fear that he might be killed and cause the collapse of their government. Once Bolívar would have flouted such orders, but he had political as well as military commitments now. Reluctantly, he turned the command of the army over to Sucre. There were protests from some of the older generals.

"I will only give my life for the Liberator!" one remonstrated.

"Then I name Antonio Sucre the Liberator and you have just given me your oath to follow him," Bolívar snapped.

For the next four months Sucre maneuvered the army through the mountain valleys and across the high plains of Peru, trying to force an encounter with the Spaniards. In December, Bolívar suffered another of the terrible coughing spells that were becoming more and more frequent. Late one night while he sat wrapped in his cape beside the stove in the cottage he shared with Manuela, a messenger burst into the room. He announced that a few days earlier, on the high plains of Ayacucho, Sucre had finally forced the Spaniards into battle. Although he had been outnumbered and the Spaniards held what appeared to be an advantageous position on the bluffs, he had routed the Spanish army completely, killing 1,500 Spanish soldiers and taking most of the others prisoners, among them the viceroy of Peru.

Bolívar leaped from his chair and began dancing on his cape. South America was free! With the Battle of Ayacucho on December 9, 1824, three hundred years of Spanish rule had ended.

Once again, Bolívar was acclaimed the hero of the hour. He was showered with gifts. Congratulations poured in from all over the world. He was elected president of Peru although he was already president of Gran Colombia. Meanwhile, Sucre led the armies into the mountainous area of what is now Bolivia, then called Alta Peru. He sent word that the people of that area wished to form an independent nation of their own to be named in the liberator's honor. Bolívar set out on a great triumphal tour, ending in Bolivia, where he wrote a constitution for the new country and witnessed the selection of Sucre as its provisional president.

For a year following the liberation of South America, Bolívar could do no wrong. Then, in 1826, everything began to turn against him. The people grumbled that he was becoming a dictator. Now that their countries were free, they wanted to organize their own governments, not those he planned for them. When Bolívar called for a general meeting of all the South American republics at Panama, only four countries sent delegates. In Gran Colombia, the quarreling between Santander and Páez reached a crisis, with Páez threatening to withdraw Venezuela from the union. When

Bolívar announced that he was returning to Gran Colombia to restore order, the people of Peru warned him that if he left them, his government there would collapse.

In Venezuela, Bolívar had no trouble bringing his old friend Páez back into line, but when he returned to Bogotá bad news waited. As he had been warned, the government of Peru had been overthrown. Before he could recover from this blow, he learned of another revolt in Bolivia, where Sucre had resigned as president and gone into retirement. For once, Bolívar was powerless to do anything, for more trouble was brewing in Colombia. During the long years Bolívar had been away fighting, Santander had replaced him in the affection of the Colombians. They were content with their old constitution and did not want the new one Bolívar proposed. When a constitutional convention resulted in a stalemate, Bolívar angrily dissolved the government and assumed the powers of dictator.

One night in Bogotá, while he lay ill in bed with Manuela reading to him, assassins broke into the palace. With Manuela's help, Bolívar escaped by jumping out of a window and hiding in the water beneath a bridge until his loyal troops could restore order. A few days later, when Bolívar was presented with a list of the plotters, Santander's name was among them. Even his old ruthlessness was fading. He ordered Santander exiled rather than executed.

Then Peru attacked Ecuador. Bolívar rode south at the head of the army again. He was in no physical condition to go into battle. He persuaded Sucre to lead the troops. Sucre successfully restored order, but it was January, 1830, before Bolívar returned to Gran Colombia. In spite of the victory, his reception was cold. The people of South America wanted peace. To them Bolívar had become a symbol of continuing war. Realizing that his popularity was gone, Bolívar resigned as dictator of Colombia.

Resignation was not enough. Fearing that his presence in South America might provoke dissension, the government ordered him into exile. Early in May he left Bogotá for the coast, where he planned to sail to Europe to find a house for himself and Manuela. As he was going down the Magdalena River, he learned that Sucre had been assassinated. It was the final tragedy. "My God, they have shed the blood of Abel!" Bolívar cried.

When he reached the coast, Bolívar was too ill to be taken aboard ship. He was carried to the plantation home of a friend on the outskirts of Santa Marta. There, attended by a physician and a few friends, he died of tuberculosis on December 17, 1830.

Bolívar's popularity was in such eclipse that he was buried quietly on the following day in a nearby churchyard. In addition to the feeling against Bolívar, a wave of nationalism was sweeping the various regions, each anxious to form its own government. Santander returned to head a new Colombian government. Páez was elected president of an independent Venezuela. Only with the passage of time were people able to remember Bolívar with less emotion, recalling his greatness as a leader and overlooking his weakness as a man. In 1842, Páez sent a naval vessel to bring Bolívar's body home. Most of the countries of the world also sent ships to act as an escort for the great naval cortege that took Bolívar back to Caracas to be reburied with honors. Today Simón Bolívar is honored throughout South America as the Great Liberator, South America's greatest hero.

7 ❧ The King Who Became Liberator

DOM PEDRO I, 1798–1834

Late in November, 1807, the port of Lisbon, Portugal, was a scene of frantic confusion, with every available sailing vessel crowded into the harbor and carts and carriages jamming the streets for blocks beyond the waterfront. Napoleon had invaded Portugal. Rather than face capture, the Portuguese royal family, along with 10,000 members of their court, lesser nobility, and their servants, were fleeing to exile in the Portuguese colony of Brazil.

Queen Maria I, who had been insane for years, was carried aboard ship by force, screaming that she was being taken to the guillotine like Marie Antoinette. From dockside her son and regent, the fat, inadequate Prince João VI, tried vainly to get some order out of chaos, while his waspish wife, Carlota, screamed in his ear that if he had any manhood he would stay and fight instead of sailing halfway around the world to some heathen colony. Surrounding them was a hubbub of voices: weeping, giving orders, cursing.

In all the melee only one person, high-spirited nine-year-old Dom Pedro, João's eldest son, seemed to be enjoying himself. His family's eviction from Europe was the most exciting event in his so-far rather dull life. Once aboard ship, while the courtiers concentrated on his demented grandmother, enraged mother, and befuddled father, he ran the decks at will, poking a curious nose into everything.

Don Pedro's exuberance did not last the trip. Off Lisbon the flotilla picked up an escort of British warships, but the crossing was rough; many of the hastily commandeered vessels were barely seaworthy; and all ran short of water. By the time they landed at Bahía, the entire royal family were ill with fever and seasickness.

After several weeks for recovery, they sailed down the coast to Rio de Janeiro, which was to be their new home and capital. The harbor, with its jutting, granite-walled Sugarloaf Mountain and curving white beach, was one of the most beautiful in the world. Viewed from the sea, its whitewashed houses spilling up the hillsides against a backdrop of lush tropical vegetation, the city looked like a paradise to the tired travelers. It was only when they went ashore that they discovered the truth. The homes of the wealthy upper classes, largely one-story buildings with thick walls, tile roofs, and narrow windows, were built around enclosed patios, only a few boasting second floors decorated with balconies. Here and there a church tower reached above the flattened city. Spreading out from these better homes, like a great muddy sea, were the ramshackle mud, wood, and thatched huts of the vast laboring class of Negroes, mulattoes, and Indians. There were no modern improvements, such as paved streets, a sewage system, or public lighting.

Making up for any disappointment in the city itself was the reception given the newcomers by the local population. Everyone of white, black, Indian, or mixed blood had turned out in his most colorful finery to see João VI, Carlota, the royal princes and princesses, and their courtiers come ashore. Not even in Portugal had the royal family ever received such homage. In the excitement and festival atmosphere, few noticed that the queen, Maria I, did not appear. Three days later, when the excitement had died down, the mad queen, disheveled, hands pressed to her face in terror, was carried ashore, placed in a carriage, and whisked off to a convent on the outskirts of town, where she would remain secluded from the public eye for the rest of her tormented life.

During the centuries since the founding of the first Portuguese settlements along the eastern coast of Brazil, Portuguese claims had spread inland far beyond the original demarcation line set by the Pope. Since most of this interior, particularly the dense jungle regions of the upper Amazon River basin, was sparsely inhabited and inaccessible to the Spanish colonies, the claim was allowed to stand. But such a huge colony, consisting of almost half of South America, was difficult to manage.

Brazil's first settlers had engaged principally in agriculture, importing huge numbers of Negro slaves to work their sugar plantations and harvest the rare hardwoods found in the jungles. Later, when gold and diamonds were discovered in the interior, more slaves were imported to work the mines, along with forced Indian labor. By the close of the eighteenth century, new plantations had been developed, raising tobacco, cacao, indigo, and cotton. With a ready supply of Negro slaves available from their African colonies, few plantation owners bothered to find those who ran away, but simply imported more to take their places. At the time of the royal family's arrival, one-half of Brazil's population of three million consisted of pure-blooded Negroes, the majority slaves, but others free men who had escaped to the interior, where they had set up small settlements of their own. Though these Negroes were poor, ill-treated, and forced to live under the most miserable conditions, by their resiliency and sheer numbers they had already made an impact on Brazil's culture, in its music, art, colorful dress, and dancing, which was loved by the entire population.

Another half million people were Indians, a few still held

in slavery, others working for meager wages in towns that had been mission settlements in the colonial days. The rest, still untouched by civilization, lived deep in the interior and upper reaches of the Amazon. The remaining third of the population was made up of the mixed breeds and a small white minority of Creole merchants, professional men, and landowners, who were the ruling class.

Portugal had attempted to follow the same shortsighted colonial policy as Spain, by imposing heavy taxes, rigid trade restrictions, and forbidding the development of independent industries in its colony. But where Spain had a strong army to enforce her harsh rule, Portugal, a much smaller nation, did not. Regulations and restrictions were often ignored or openly flouted.

Portuguese administrators sent to Brazil found it virtually impossible to control such a vast, sprawling colony. They collected what they could for the king and forgot the rest. Brazilians might grumble about their taxes, but they did not suffer greatly. When the royal family sought sanctuary in Brazil, the people were ready to accept them open heartedly.

In Portugal, João had been an ineffective regent, secretly laughed at by many of his courtiers and completely dominated by his wife, Carlota, the strong-willed, hot-tempered daughter of the King of Spain. In Brazil, greeted by a population that seemed to genuinely respect him, the regent found new vigor. The reception genuinely touched him, and he instituted a new era of reform. He did away with the Portuguese monopoly on trade and opened Brazil's ports to all foreign vessels. He began a vigorous campaign to modernize Rio de Janeiro, improving the harbor, paving the streets, importing printing presses for a newspaper, and founding a military academy, the first bank, public library, museum, and a botanical garden that would soon become world famous. In 1816, when the demented Maria I died and he was crowned King João VI, he chose to remain in Brazil instead of returning to Portugal.

Carlota shared none of her husband's enthusiasm for Brazil. She had the typical European disdain for anyone from the colonies. After Napoleon marched into Spain also, dethroning her father, Charles IV, then her brother Ferdinand, she entered into countless intrigues, attempting to be declared empress of all the Spanish colonies of South America. Just as the Brazilians loved gentle King João, they hated Carlota, who liked to gallop through the streets in a careening carriage, accompanied by a private bodyguard equipped with whips to deal with any colonist who hesitated to drop to his knees as she passed.

Between his father's absorption in civic reforms and his mother's interest in political intrigues, young Dom Pedro received almost no parental supervision. He was a handsome boy with curly dark hair, flashing eyes, and, to his mother's horror, completely democratic ways. He loved horses and spent a great deal of his time with the palace stableman. He roamed the palace at will, but frequently slipped out into the streets, where the horrified servants would find him playing with the ragged street urchins.

As a boy, Dom Pedro disliked the pomp and ceremony of state functions. One of his favorite tricks, when he became bored at one of these formal affairs, was to wait until a young noble of his own age had bent over his hand to give it the usual kiss; then he would double his fist and give the startled youth a clout on the chin. From the time he reached his teens he was choosing his own friends and expressing his own ideas. He delighted in riding about the streets alone, talking to everyone. As he grew older, he scandalized, yet delighted, the Brazilians with his youthful escapades.

King João was too weak to control his son, and in time even Carlota tired of trying to correct him. Instead she devoted all of her attention to rearing Dom Pedro's younger brother, Dom Miguel, to be an arrogant replica of herself.

When Dom Pedro was nineteen his family arranged an advantageous marriage for him with the Archduchess Leopoldina of the powerful Austrian Hapsburgs. A stocky, athletic girl with blonde hair and a cheerful smile, Leopoldina was no beauty, but she was extremely intelligent. She immediately won King João's heart with her mutual interest in horticulture. She won the hearts of the Brazilians also for her democratic ways and friendliness. She was a splendid horsewoman, and dressed in the blue and gold uniform of the dragoons, she often reviewed the troops beside her husband, much to the delight of the people.

Whether Leopoldina won the heart of Dom Pedro remained a question. There seemed little doubt that she fell in love with the handsome prince, and Dom Pedro respected her intelligence and depended on her judgment, but he had already engaged in several torrid love affairs and would have others. A year and a half after their marriage, Leopoldina gave birth to a daughter, Maria da Gloria, but two sons born over the next two years died in infancy.

King João's popularity, which had reached its height during the first seven or eight years of his exile, slowly began to decline after 1816. His expensive building program meant added taxation. At his wife's instigation he engaged in a costly and unpopular border war with Argentina. Moreover, Napoleon had been defeated in Europe and there were repeated demands for him to return to Portugal, which was being ruled by a regency in his absence.

Sparked by the struggle for independence being carried on around them by the Spanish colonies of South America, a movement for independence had begun to stir in Brazil also. A minor revolt was put down in one of the provinces, but the next revolutionary news came from Portugal itself, where some of the king's own soldiers had started a revolt calling for an overthrow of the regency and summoning a 200-member *cortes* to set up a constitutional monarchy like England's. When the news reached Brazil, there was street rioting, and a contingent of João's own Portuguese followers joined Brazilians in demanding that this same constitutional monarchy be extended to Brazil. It is reported that João's first reaction on hearing of the rebellion was to faint. However, he quickly recovered when he learned that his life and his throne were not threatened. He agreed to the adoption of the new constitution and in April, 1820, with the grimly triumphant Carlota beside him, he set sail for Portugal to make his peace with the new *cortes*.

Dom Miguel, the rest of Dom Pedro's brothers and sisters, the Portuguese nobles, and all their servants followed the king, so that Rio de Janeiro was the scene of a mass exodus on a fleet of hastily assembled ships as large as the fleet that had brought the royal court to Brazil ten years earlier. Only Dom Pedro was left behind, with a small supporting army to continue to rule as prince regent and viceroy of Brazil. In spite of his weaknesses as a monarch, João VI loved Brazil dearly. Before he sailed, he took his eldest son aside, telling him that if the move for independence sweeping the Spanish colonies should spread to Brazil, he was free to follow his own inclinations and go along with his adopted people rather than plunge Brazil into war.

Once his father had gone, the twenty-two-year-old regent was overwhelmed with problems. João VI had issued paper money to cover his elaborate building schemes. Fearing it would have no value in Europe, the returning Portuguese courtiers had cashed this paper for silver and gold at the local banks, leaving the country almost bankrupt. The people were already grumbling about new taxes to support a European government. A few of the more independent provinces even refused to recognize Dom Pedro's regency. Worst of all, when Dom Pedro finally heard from his father after the long voyage, he suspected that João's letters were being censored by someone. Pedro was ready to sail for Portugal to help his father, but Leopoldina urged him to stay. Added to her influence was that of José Bonifácio de Andrada, a brilliant professor and leader of the independence movement, who pointed out that Dom Pedro's interests lay with Brazil now, not Portugal.

Dom Pedro needed their support. As he had feared, his weak father had become the tool of the powerful Portuguese *cortes*. Soon Dom Pedro received an order to return home to "complete his education." In desperation he wrote his father and the *cortes* a letter signed in his own blood stating that he continued loyal to Portugal. The result was another, even more demanding, order for his return.

"Your departure would be the signal for rebellion. . . . With you as leader, we will remain united and victorious," Bonifácio told him.

On January 9, 1822, Dom Pedro issued a proclamation to the people of Brazil, saying that for the good of all and the general well-being of the nation, he had decided to remain. "I remain Day" is still celebrated as a national holiday in Brazil.

Portuguese troops stationed in the capital immediately marched to seize Dom Pedro and Leopoldina to send them back to Portugal by force; but a people's army gathered to block their way. Men and women armed themselves with guns, knives, and cudgels. Priests joined them, carrying blunderbusses. Leopoldina managed to escape to their country home, where only a few weeks later she gave birth to another daughter; but Dom Pedro remained in the city.

His show of strength finally quieted the troops, and on February 15, 1822, he was sworn into office as the "Emperor and Perpetual Defender of Brazil." According to the constitutional monarchy proposed by the Brazilians, Brazil was to become a commonwealth, which would have its own government but give final allegiance to Portugal. In an effort to consolidate the entire country, Dom Pedro set off on a trip through the provinces to reassure the people.

He was hardly on his way before a reply came from the *cortes* in the form of a squadron of Portuguese warships. A courtier brought a message ashore. Leopoldina read it, then called a meeting of her husband's ministers. This time the Portuguese *cortes* was not quibbling. Dom Pedro was ordered to start home in thirty days, and an appointed governor was being sent to take his place. Leopoldina sent the message on to her husband, accompanied by a note of her own: "The apple is ripe. Harvest it now or it will rot!"

The mail reached Dom Pedro on September 7, 1822, as he traveled along a back-country trail near the Ypiranga River. Riding a short distance away from his soldiers, he broke the seals and read the messages. As the others watched in astonishment, he suddenly ripped the Portuguese insignia from his uniform and threw it to the ground. Raising his sword, he whirled around. "Off with the Portuguese colors," he ordered. "By the blood which flows in my veins, I swear to free Brazil. Independence or death! We are separated from Portugal!"

"Independence or death!" the cry swept like a great wave across all of Brazil. This *Grito de Ypiranga*, or "Cry of Ypiranga," was Brazil's declaration of independence, and September 7 is celebrated as Brazil's Independence Day.

A month later, on October 22, 1822, his twenty-fifth birthday, Dom Pedro was named Pedro I, constitutional emperor of Brazil. The flag of Portugal was hauled down and replaced by the new green, gold, and blue flag of Brazil. During the ceremonies Dom Pedro wore an armband bearing the legend: "Independence or Death." He asked all who favored his government to do the same. Overnight the nation, fifth largest in the world in land size, came alive with the slogan— scribbled on walls, sewn on banners, displayed on the arms of citizens.

There was no more talk of a commonwealth. The new and independent government was designed as an independent constitutional monarchy with two houses: a lower house of elected representatives and an upper house of senators, appointed for life. The king was given the power to dissolve congress and veto laws of which he did not approve.

After the declaration, the Portuguese navy attempted to blockade Brazilian ports, but Dom Pedro secured the services of Admiral Cochrane, the same renegade British officer who had helped San Martín and O'Higgins in Chile and Peru. Using only small ships, Cochrane successfully broke the blockade. There was some very minor land fighting, but nothing to compare with the violent fighting that marked the struggle of the Spanish colonies. Within three years Brazil was completely free of Portugal, with almost no bloodshed.

In 1824, the United States recognized Brazil's independence, followed by Great Britain in 1825. Dom Pedro's rule was not easy. In his youth he had been very liberal, but once he became emperor he began to change. He had been spoiled as a boy by people who indulged every whim; now as a man

DOM PEDRO I

he could not stand criticism. Many Brazilians were afraid that Dom Pedro still took orders from Portugal. In return, he became even more resentful of any criticism of his appointments, particularly those of Portuguese citizens.

Less than a year after the declaration of independence, after hearing that congress had criticized two of his appointees for engaging in a street fight with a native, Dom Pedro rode on horseback to the building where the body was meeting. He trained a cannon on the entrance and, striding inside, used his prerogative to order congress dismissed.

One of those leaving the chamber was the brother of Dom Pedro's old supporter José Bonifácio de Andrada. As he came down the steps, he removed his hat and made a mocking bow, not to the king but to the cannon. "My respects to your majesty," he said.

Infuriated by such insolence, Dom Pedro ordered the entire Andrada family exiled. Within a short time his rage subsided and he presided at the drafting of a new and even more liberal constitution. But the damage had been done. In José Bonifácio, Dom Pedro had lost one of his staunchest supporters; and he also lost the faith of many of the people.

Though Dom Pedro had arrived in Brazil as a small boy, the fact that he had been born in Portugal was enough to make many Brazilians suspicious of his loyalties. Many people felt that they could accept a king wholeheartedly only if he were native born. Following the death of their two infant sons, Leopoldina had borne three more children, all girls. In 1825, she was pregnant again. As the time for her confinement drew near, the entire nation waited anxiously. Early on the morning of December 2, the thunder of the palace cannons announced a royal birth. People rushed into the street to watch the night sky for the signal: two rockets for a girl, three for a boy. Two rockets climbed above the palace;

there was a long pause, then a third exploded above the others and the citizens went wild with joy. They had a potential king of true Brazilian birth, Dom Pedro II!

Within days after the infant's birth, elaborate ceremonies were held, guaranteeing his succession to the throne. His prestige briefly restored by this display of national rejoicing, Dom Pedro I set out on another tour of the country.

In the spring of the following year King João VI of Portugal died. All of Brazil waited to see whether Dom Pedro I would return to Europe to become Pedro IV of Portugal. Dom Pedro sought to prove his loyalty by announcing his abdication of the Portuguese throne, but he named his seven-year-old daughter, Maria da Gloria, as his successor and the queen of Portugal. The decision was unexpected. His ambitious mother and most of the Portuguese nobility had believed he would abdicate in favor of his brother Dom Miguel. When there were protests from Portugal, Dom Pedro tried to mend political fences by announcing the betrothal of little Maria to her uncle. Such inter-family marriages were not uncommon in Europe, where preservation of the throne was considered of first importance. To the less-sophisticated Brazilians, the whole affair had an unsavory air of political intrigue.

As a youth, Dom Pedro had amused his indulgent subjects with his numerous romantic attachments; but they were not as lenient when they came to love the homely but faithful Leopoldina. As long as Dom Pedro kept his infidelities secret, scandal was kept to a minimum. When he openly took a new mistress, built her an elaborate palace, and made her a member of his ruling council, more people turned against him. In 1862, when Leopoldina suddenly became ill and died while Dom Pedro was away on another tour of the country, there were rumors that Leopoldina had really died of a broken heart. Following her death, it seemed as though Dom Pedro could do nothing right. He sent his mistress into exile and sought to appease the people by marrying the Princess Amelia of Leuchtenberg. But a new spirit of nationalism was rising all over Brazil. The Brazilians wanted no connection with Portugal. Dom Pedro, by declaring his little daughter queen of Portugal, had reinforced those ties. Accompanied by Amelia, Dom Pedro started another tour of the provinces, but was met with such a cold reception that he returned home without completing the trip.

On his return, the reception at Rio de Janeiro was equally unenthusiastic. Angered by what they considered an insult to their emperor, the Portuguese-born mercantile section of town set off its own celebration with fireworks, bonfires in the streets, and shouts of "Down with the Brazilians." No move could have been more unfortunate. The infuriated native population marched on the waterfront area, where the Portuguese merchants drove them back after bloody street fighting, many using broken wine bottles from their shops as their weapons. The action, referred to as *Noite de Garrafadas*, or "Night of the Bottles," in Brazilian history, marked the end of Dom Pedro's reign.

Within days most of the citizens were wearing armbands of yellow and green again. This time they were a symbol of dissatisfaction with Dom Pedro's rule. On August 6, 1831, angry mobs began to assemble in the streets. While Dom Pedro and his family watched in dismay, government troops began to join them. Dom Pedro stood at a palace window watching the distant mob through field glasses. Below him, he saw his own Imperial Guard ride away from the palace; following them were his aides, finally even his servants. Early on the morning of April 7, Dom Pedro signed papers of abdication in favor of his son, Dom Pedro II.

When they were told the news, the crowds were overjoyed. The tiny five-year-old king was led to a balcony, where he was placed on a chair so that the people could see him from below. Brazil had a new and native-born king.

While the five-year-old monarch was being acclaimed by the crowd, his father, stepmother, and oldest sister, Maria, were sailing out of the Rio de Janeiro harbor aboard a British warship. Dom Pedro had left behind his four other daughters to be companions for his young son, so that the small king would not have to grow up alone, isolated from loved ones. He also wrote to José Bonifácio to return and supervise the education of his son. By renouncing the throne, Dom Pedro had insured the continuance of the Brazilian monarchy for another generation.

In Europe, Dom Pedro found that his mother and brother had conspired to seize the throne of Portugal, calling off the betrothal with Maria, the rightful queen. Dom Pedro's final years were spent fighting for his daughter's rights. From France he led a successful expedition into Portugal and saw his daughter crowned Queen Maria II, but he contracted tuberculosis during the long, arduous campaign. On September 24, 1834, only a short time after her coronation, Dom Pedro I died in Portugal.

Like many of the other liberators, Dom Pedro appeared to end his life in tragedy. However, he had brought about the liberation of Brazil without bloodshed, placed his son on the throne of Brazil, his daughter on the throne of Portugal, and had maintained amicable relations between the mother country and the former colony, something the Spanish colonies would not achieve for generations.

8 ❈ *El Grito*

MIGUEL HIDALGO, 1753–1811

In the Spanish colonies of South America, the struggle for independence had its beginning in the cities. In Mexico it began as a rural movement. Part of this difference was because Mexico had a much larger Spanish-born population than the other colonies, but also because its colonial development had been somewhat different.

With the exception of the Incas of Peru, most of the Indian tribes of the South American colonies were extremely backward and primitive. However, when the Spanish conquistadors of Hernando Cortés landed in Mexico, they found the Mexican Indians were already skilled farmers. Because of their more advanced civilization, they had been much more willing to accept Christianity, and thousands of missionary priests had flocked into Mexico to conduct this work of conversion. With the help of the Indians, more than twelve hundred churches were built in Mexico during the colonial period and the Catholic Church in Mexico became tremendously powerful, both in wealth and influence.

Slavery was introduced in Mexico but it did not flourish. With a huge, docile force of Christianized Indians to work on their haciendas and in their mines, the wealthy landowning Creoles did not need to import slaves. By the start of the wars of independence the population of Mexico, like that of most of the other colonies, was divided into two major classes: the landowning clergy and white Creoles, who were enormously wealthy; and the landless, laboring

Indians and mestizos, who barely survived in their poverty.

The Indians made up the largest segment of the population. In return for a tribute to the king of one *peso* a year, they were supposed to be free men, but they lived only one step from slavery. They were required to dwell in segregated villages of their own. There they lived in clusters of crude mud or adobe huts with thatched roofs and worked in communal fields alloted to each village. They were forbidden to wear European clothes. The women usually dressed in full cotton skirts and blouses, the men in baggy white cotton pantaloons and shirts, with square *ponchos* of woven wool or manguey fiber for warmth. They were not allowed to own horses, since these were considered the exclusive property of the Europeans; so they plowed their fields by hand, planting the maize, which was their staple food, by pushing seeds into the ground with pointed sticks. Though the Indians were supposedly free men, whenever labor was needed for the mines or construction of a public building, the white administrator of the district could conscript as many Indian workers as were needed.

Mestizos lived under conditions that were only slightly better than those of the Indians. They were forbidden to live in the Indian villages, but they were not accepted by the whites. Many lived in shabby suburbs of the cities, where they worked as semiskilled workers or helpers in the shops. Others worked in the country as foremen in the mines or on the ranches.

The schools, all of which were operated by the Church, were not for the Indians. They catered principally to the children of the white Creoles, though occasionally, if a mestizo could raise the money for tuition, he could acquire a little education and better himself by slipping into some very minor government office or into lower position in the clergy.

Although they were wealthy and seemed to hold a favored position, the landowning Creoles did not occupy the top rung of the social ladder in Mexico as they did in the other colonies. This position was reserved exclusively for those who had been born in Spain. Called derisively *gapuchines* (translated literally to mean "wearers of spurs"), this Spanish segment of the population was hated almost universally by Indians, mestizos, and Creoles.

Mexico's wealth in silver, the bustling activity of her port cities on both the Atlantic and Pacific coasts, plus the fine, healthful climate of Mexico City in the interior, made Mexico much more attractive than the other colonies to Spanish adventurers who wanted to spend only a short time in the New World to make a fortune. The majority of federal, state, and even municipal offices were held by these *gapuchine* administrators, many of whom had secured their appointments by bribery or outright gifts to the king. In addition, in the coastal cities almost all business and trade were controlled by Spanish merchants and importers.

In 1809, when the news of Charles IV's abdication and the advance of Napoleon into Spain reached Mexico City, the reaction of the Creoles was the same as it had been in the other colonies. They immediately began to talk of setting up a government of their own in the name of Ferdinand VII. But the huge body of *gapuchines* were not about to be ejected from their lucrative offices. Assisted by the Spanish army, they acted first, imprisoning the known Creole liberals and taking over the government themselves in order to insure its loyalty to Spain. Instead of becoming the seat of the revolution, Mexico City became the stronghold of Spanish power. If there were to be any move for independence, it would have to find leaders somewhere out in the rural areas.

At fifty-seven years of age, thin, stoop shouldered, with a fringe of wispy white hair edging a bulbous bald head, Father Miguel Hidalgo hardly presented the heroic figure expected of a revolutionary leader. But almost from the day of his birth, May 8, 1753, in the province of Guanajuato, northwest of Mexico City, he had been preparing himself for the decision he was to make.

Hidalgo's parents were of upper-middle-class Creole stock, his father being the manager of a large hacienda. When Hidalgo was twelve, he and an older brother were sent to a Jesuit school in the city of Valladolid (now Morelia). A year later, when this Jesuit seminary was closed, the two boys were transferred to another school in Valladolid, the College of San Nicolás, where Hidalgo was to remain for the next twenty-five years, as student, teacher, treasurer, and finally head of the institution. As a student, Hidalgo distinguished himself for his brilliance, particularly in the art of debate, winning the nickname, "The Fox," for his cleverness. During this period the American Revolution took place, and though most of the supposedly inflammatory writings of the French and American writers were banned by the Church, it was not difficult for young intellectuals like Hidalgo to obtain smuggled copies.

Once he became an educator, Hidalgo distinguished himself as a liberal. In those days, when the Church offered one of the few careers open to men of learning, piety was not a prerequisite for priesthood. Like many of his fellow priests, Hidalgo was fond of music, dancing, and gambling, and was the father of several illegitimate children. But in time, his liberal ideas proved to be the undoing of his career as an educator. As a teacher, then treasurer, of San Nicolás, his

MIGUEL HIDALGO

work was proficient; but once elevated to the top post of rector, he initiated such a costly program to liberalize the curriculum that he ran the college into debt and was replaced.

For the next ten years, Hidalgo served as a parish priest. During those years, the French Revolution added fuel to his ideas of personal and political freedom. One of his rectories was given the nickname "Little France" because its doors were open to all and it was the constant setting for dances, musicals, and the debates on political themes that Hidalgo loved so dearly. Not everyone shared his outspoken ideas. In 1800, two visiting priests were sufficiently shocked by Hidalgo's opinions to report him to the Office of the Inquisition. Fortunately, Hidalgo had influential friends and was cleared of the charges, but the incident taught him a lesson. After that he kept his ideas to himself except among those he could trust.

In 1803 Hidalgo took over the parish of Dolores, vacated by the death of his older brother. Once again the doors of the rectory were open to everyone, but now Hidalgo's interest shifted from intellectual pursuits to the work of improving the lives of the Otomi Indians, who formed the majority of his parish.

Sending for books on subjects he had never studied before, Hidalgo instructed the Indians in bee-keeping, wine-making, and silkworm culture. He set up factories, forges, and workshops, where he taught them to tan leather, forge simple tools, make bricks, and manufacture the Otomi pottery for which that district is still famous. His work won him the devotion of the Indians but brought him again to the unfavorable attention of the authorities. Under the Spanish policy forbidding any colonial industry competitive with Spanish trade, both wine-making and silk production were illegal.

Soldiers were sent to cut down his vines and mulberry bushes, though Hidalgo himself was not arrested.

Hidalgo still enjoyed the companionship of other liberal thinkers in spite of the long hours he spent with his Indian industries. Dolores was a rural parish, so in order to find intellectual companionship he rode 50 miles to the city of Querétaro. His frequent companions on these trips were Ignacio Allende—a Creole landowner and captain of the militia at the town of San Miguel, located midway between Dolores and Querétaro—and one of Allende's junior officers, Juan Aldama. In the city they met at the home of the town *corregidor*, or "administrator," with other Creoles of the area who shared their liberal opinions.

News of Napoleon's march into Spain, followed by the seizure of the government in Mexico City by the *gapuchines*, was a devastating blow to them all. Where Hidalgo's previous liberal companions had been other priests and scholars, who liked to talk about theories, his new companions were Creole landowners and militia officers, who were men of action as well as words. With no hope that a revolution would be launched by the imprisoned liberals of Mexico City, they decided to organize one of their own.

Forewarned by what had happened to the Creoles in the capital, they worked in secret. In his workshops at Dolores, Hidalgo had his Indians fashion spears, machetes, and knives. He sent away for books on manufacturing gunpowder and forging cannon. Meanwhile, Allende and Aldama contacted Creole officers in other towns, urging them to join the movement. The revolt was scheduled for the first of October, 1810, when most of the people would be assembled for a district fair, but as more and more people became involved in the plot, it became more difficult to keep it secret.

News of the plan finally reached Mexico City. On September 15, Spanish soldiers rode into Querétaro, taking over the home of the town's *corregidor*. There was nothing the official could do without betraying his own involvement, but his wife managed to slip out of the house and send a rider to warn the others.

It was early morning when the horseman finally galloped into Dolores, where Allende had been spending the night. Immediately he, Aldama, and the others rushed to awaken Hidalgo at the rectory.

"Gentlemen, we are lost!" Hidalgo cried. Then out of desperation he seemed to find resolve. "Come, there is no other course than to attack the *gapuchines* now!"

Startled by the sudden transformation in the priest, the others agreed. It was only a matter of hours before their part in the plot would be known. At the Dolores jail, Hidalgo ordered the release of all prisoners. Daylight was creeping across the hills. It was Sunday, and many Indians and their families were already arriving in town to attend church. Hidalgo ordered the church bells rung. When the Indians had gathered, he told them what had happened. "Will you live under tyranny and bad government forever or will you join with us."

"Down with bad government!" was the resounding cry of hundreds of voices. The Indians summoned friends and gathered their homemade weapons. By the time they left Dolores for San Miguel, where they would pick up Allende's men, their army already numbered close to a thousand.

On the way they passed a small hamlet, its tiny cluster of huts overshadowed by the ruins of an abandoned Jesuit Church. While the marchers rested, Hidalgo entered the sanctuary to pray. As he was leaving, he tore a banner of the

Virgin of Guadalupe, patroness saint of Mexico, from the wall. The Lady of Guadalupe became the symbol for the revolution. As the march continued, Hidalgo rode ahead, dressed in his black knee breeches, long frock coat, and round-brimmed curate's hat, holding the banner aloft. Attracted by the procession, Indians along the way snatched up machetes or pitchforks and joined them.

At San Miguel there was no opposition as Allende's militia and most of the men of the town gathered their arms and joined the rebel army. On September 19, the town of Celaya fell to the revolutionists; but for the first time, Hidalgo and Allende lost control of their army as their ragged troops ran through the streets robbing, burning, and pillaging. When they continued from Celaya, headed for the state capital, Guanajuato, the rebel army numbered 25,000.

Hidalgo had exchanged the black garb of a priest for the uniform of the militia and had assumed military leadership, with Allende next in command. Leading the army were priests carrying the banners of the Lady of Guadalupe. Next came Hidalgo in his new uniform, then Allende and the blue and-white-clad militia, and finally the great, stumbling, crowding mass of Indians and mestizos in their white cotton pantaloons and woven ponchos. Many of the Indians carried paintings, chairs, clothing, and other loot on their heads or shoulders. Others waved crude little hand-painted banners of the Lady of Guadalupe. Behind them trailed many of their wives and children.

Guanajuato, a major mining center of some 65,000 people, was situated in a deep defile between the mountains that made it almost impossible to defend. During the night, the governor gathered the town's leading *gapuchine* and Creole citizens. With the protection of the local militia, they gath-

Statue of Hidalgo carrying the banner of the Virgin of Guadalupe

ered their most valuable possessions and took refuge in the huge fortresslike granary, the *Alhóndiga de Granaditas,* in the center of town, believing they could hold out there until Spanish troops arrived to help them. Politically it was a terrible mistake. In the morning, when they discovered how they had been betrayed by their leaders and the upper classes, the remainder of the townspeople went over to Hidalgo's side.

Pressing into town in a sea of human bodies, the rebel army surrounded the granary. Those who could not find room on the streets, climbed the hills and threw stones down on the building, so that soon its roof was covered to a depth of one foot. For a time the troops inside were able to turn back the rebels, killing them by the hundreds. But others climbed forward over their bodies to continue the assault. Finally a miner, protected from the soldiers' bullets by a stone slab on his shoulders, managed to set the door of the granary afire. The mob burst through the still-blazing door, killing and butchering everyone they found. By the time Allende's soldiers could club their way inside, only a handful of survivors remained to be taken prisoner.

Their rage still unsated, the mob turned on the town, looting and burning. Others swarmed into the hills, where they smashed and destroyed the valuable machinery of the mines. The looting and revelry continued throughout the night. Hidalgo took the philosophical attitude that pillage was a necessary accompaniment of victory; but Allende, accustomed to handling well-disciplined soldiers, was appalled. The revolution was not going at all as it had been planned at Querétaro. It was to have been a well-organized display of Creole strength; instead it was turning into a vendetta of the lower classes. Few of the peasant soldiers could tell the difference between Creoles and *gapuchines*. Creole homes and lives were being destroyed along with those of the hated Spaniards.

Leaving a semblance of government to preside over the ruins, Hidalgo pressed on to Valladolid, where he had spent so many years at the College of San Nicolás. News of the sack of Guanajuato had raced ahead of him. On October 17, Valladolid surrendered without a fight on the promise that the city would be spared.

Word of Hidalgo's famous *grito*, or "cry," of Dolores had spread throughout most of Mexico. Hidalgo sent volunteers into other areas to arouse the people to join his crusade. But no revolution erupted in Mexico City. Instead, Church officials labeled Hidalgo a heretic and ordered his excommunication. At the outbreak of the revolution General Felix Calleja, commander of the Spanish army in Mexico, was stationed with most of his troops at San Luis Potosí far to the north. Hidalgo's rabble army was moving with such speed that before Calleja could get south, they were already heading from Valladolid toward Mexico City, which was practically undefended.

The capital of Mexico was located in a high valley completely surrounded by mountains. The Spanish soldiers in the city, reinforced by Creole volunteers, mustered an army of about 2,500 men, who set up their cannon to meet Hidalgo's army of 65,000 at one of the passes leading into the valley. It was the first time Hidalgo's soldiers had faced organized resistance or seen a cannon. In their ignorance, some of the peasants attempted to silence the big guns by putting their sombreros over the muzzles. After 2,000 of Hidalgo's men had been killed, the others pushed through the pass, forcing the defenders to flee back to Mexico City.

That night Hidalgo made camp inside the Valley of Mexico. Ahead the capital lay defenseless, but abruptly Hidalgo changed his mind. Possibly, he realized that if his army were turned loose in the capital in an orgy of looting and drunkenness, he could never reassemble them in time to defend the city when Calleja arrived.

Against the advice of the other officers, Hidalgo led the army back over the mountains just in time to meet Calleja, riding south with 7,000 soldiers. Hidalgo's peasants had just seen 2,000 of their comrades killed. They had little stomach for going back into battle so soon. After only a pretense of fighting, they disbanded and fled. In the ensuing disorder the army split, some fleeing with Allende to Guanajuato, the rest with Hidalgo to Valladolid.

Nothing could have pleased Calleja more. Now it was Allende who must defend Guanajuato against an invading army. Deciding the risks were too great, he ordered the remaining Spanish prisoners executed and fled west to the town of Guadalajara, where he was joined by Hidalgo. While Hidalgo set up an independent government, Allende began the task of reorganizing their undisciplined army.

Hidalgo's government, like the first governments set up in the other colonies, did not call for a completely independent Mexico, but merely an independent congress to rule until Ferdinand VII could be restored to the throne. In a periodical called *Despertador Americano*, he published political theories calling for the liberation of all slaves and freeing of the Indians from paying their annual tribute to the crown.

In January, 1811, word reached Hidalgo that General Calleja was marching on Guadalajara. Though Allende had been drilling and training their men, only one soldier out of ten was equipped with firearms, the rest carrying only spears, slings, bows and arrows, or machetes. Allende recommended that they employ guerrilla tactics. But Hidalgo had such faith that his army of 70,000 could overrun Calleja's 10,000 men, that he ordered them out of the city to meet the enemy on the open plains where the bridge of Calderón crossed the Lerma River.

The armies met on January 17, and for a time Hidalgo's faith seemed justified, as his native soldiers held their ground and even began to force the soldiers back. Then a Spanish artillery shell hit an ammunition cart at the rear of Hidalgo's forces. Moments later a grass fire ignited by the exploding ammunition swept down on the rebel troops. Caught between the advancing flames and the Spaniards, the terrorized soldiers tried to flee. The battle became a rout. Thousands were slaughtered, while those fortunate enough to escape into the hills, threw away their weapons and headed back to their homes, tired of fighting and the revolution.

Hidalgo and Allende escaped, but the following day, when they attempted to reassemble their forces at a ranch house in the north, their army of 70,000 had been reduced to 2,000. Hidalgo was stripped of leadership, and Allende was chosen to take his place. With Calleja close on their heels, they headed north to the town of Saltillo, where a young Creole officer named Mariano Jiménez had staged one of the many successful local revolutions. In order to take Saltillo, Jiménez had used the help of a militia officer to whom he had promised promotion to a high office in the rebel army. When Allende and Hidalgo reached Saltillo with their weary men, they were in no mood to talk promotions, and Allende dismissed the militia officer summarily. This proved to be a mistake even more fatal than those made by Hidalgo.

Unable to reorganize their army at Saltillo, they fled north again, hoping this time to reach sanctuary across the United States border. But the disgruntled militia officer betrayed their route to the Spaniards. On a lonely stretch of desert, Hidalgo, Allende, and their few remaining men were ambushed and captured.

The leaders were taken to Chihuahua, the capital of that northern region, where after a brief military trial, Allende, Aldama, and Jiménez were convicted of treason and executed before a firing squad.

Hidalgo's trial took longer, for first he had to be tried by the Church. For days he cleverly matched wits with his inquisitors, but in the end the mental torture forced him to partially recant. He refused to denounce the revolution or the principles for which it stood, but he did ask pardon for the bloodshed, devastation, and thousands of lives that had been needlessly sacrificed.

On July 30, he was led into the courtyard of the former Jesuit college that had served as his prison. After distributing a few candies to the members of the firing squad and giving them his forgiveness, he went calmly to his death. Following the executions, the heads of Hidalgo, Allende, Aldama, and Jiménez were severed and placed in iron cages. Taken to Guanajuato, they were hung at the four corners of the granary *Alhóndiga de Granaditas*, as a grisly warning to others who might be tempted to plot against the government.

Today Hidalgo is revered as the "Father of Mexican Independence." September 16, the anniversary of his *Grito de Dolores*, is a national holiday. His body, exhumed from the plot at Chihuahua, rests in the capital beside those of other patriots.

9 ▦ The Soldier Priest

JOSÉ MORELOS, 1765–1815

The death of Father Hidalgo failed to snuff out the fire of freedom in Mexico. For the remainder of 1811, General Calleja and the Spanish army were kept busy, stamping out the remaining sparks of rebellion in the towns north of the capital, which had supported the revolution. While the Spaniards were thus engaged in the north, the revolution flared up again, this time in the south, led by another priest, José Morelos, who, because of his humble background seemed to be an even less likely candidate for leadership than his predecessor.

José María Morelos was born on September 30, 1765, in the city of Valladolid to impoverished mestizo parents. Only the fact that his mother was the daughter of a schoolteacher enabled him to learn to read and write, for his family was much too poor to send him to school. When Morelos was fourteen his father died and the youth was sent south to work for an uncle, since he was then the sole support of his mother and sister.

Acapulco was Mexico's leading port on the Pacific coast. It was there that the Spanish ships brought their rich cargoes from the Orient, which were loaded on muleback and taken up a winding road through the mountains to Mexico City in the interior. Morelos worked first as a plantation laborer, later as a muleteer on the so-called "China Road" that led from Acapulco to the capital. The work was hard and exhausting, but it toughened his body and gave him an intimate knowledge of the rough mountain region southwest of the capital.

Morelos had no intention of remaining a mule skinner forever. In addition to the money he sent to his mother, he was able to put enough aside so that when he was twenty-five he quit his job and returned to Valladolid, where he entered the College of San Nicolás to study for the priesthood. During this time, Father Hidalgo took over as rector, but Morelos was of such unprepossessing appearance that it is doubtful that Hidalgo noticed him among the other students.

Morelos was barely five feet tall, of stocky build with coarse black hair, a swarthy complexion, thick lips, and a face disfigured by both smallpox and an ugly scar across the bridge of his nose, resulting from a boyhood accident. Taciturn and grimly serious, he almost never smiled. He mingled little with the other students, devoting his college years to attaining the priesthood as quickly as possible before his limited funds were exhausted.

In 1797, his goal was achieved. Ordained a priest, Morelos was assigned to a poor Indian parish northwest of Acapulco. His mother, who accompanied him as his housekeeper, had always lived in the cool mountain air of Valladolid. When she became ill in the sultry, semitropical climate, Morelos asked for a transfer to a better parish. The reward for such effrontery was his transfer to an ever poorer parish in the equally humid climate at Carácuaro. By the time the orders came, Morelos' mother had already died. He accepted the change without complaint, but the first seeds of bitterness against the Church had been planted.

In the following years as Morelos labored at his parish without advancement, he learned more about the position those of mixed blood held in the Church hierarchy. His

JOSÉ MORELOS

parish was so poor that he was forced to raise cattle just to supply his own needs. Stern and demanding, he was admired more than loved by his parishoners. After ten years at Carácuaro, Morelos realized that he would probably spend his entire life at the same miserable little parish, for only those of pure blood had any chance of advancement in the Church. As before, he kept his dissatisfaction hidden until October, 1810, when the first word of Hidalgo's *Grito de Dolores* reached Carácuaro. Morelos' imagination was fired by the movement, but there seemed to be little he or his small parish could do to help. Then, on October 13, he received orders from the bishop to publish the bans for Hidalgo's excommunication. Unable to bring himself to take such a drastic step, he hurried north to talk to Hidalgo himself.

By the time Morelos reached Hidalgo's camp, the revolutionary army had left Valladolid and was marching toward Mexico City. Hidalgo refused Morelos' offer to join his army as a chaplain, explaining he already had too many chaplains. Instead he suggested that Morelos return to Carácuaro, raise an army of peasants, and march on Acapulco.

It did not matter that Morelos had neither money nor military training. As a youth of fourteen he had been penniless and uneducated, yet he had become a priest. Armed with only his determination, Morelos returned to Carácuaro. His initial efforts were not encouraging. In his own parish he was able to raise only 25 men, but on October 25, he set off with this small company for Acapulco. Word of the revolution had spread ahead of him. As Morelos moved south, Indians left their villages, Negroes and mestizos left their plantation jobs to join him. In less than a month, Morelos was approaching Acapulco at the head of an army of over 2,000 men.

The port city curved around a half-moon bay, defended on its outer perimeter by the well-fortified garrisons of a number of suburbs, with another huge fortress, mounting 100 heavy cannon, as its inner defense. Morelos' men captured several suburbs, but their cannon, which were mostly small salute guns picked up at villages along the way, were powerless against the 12-foot-thick walls of the inner fortress.

Failing in a direct assault, Morelos spread his forces through the hills and laid siege to the city. Recruits continued to pour into his camp until his army numbered 9,000. But the siege was fruitless, for Spanish ships kept Acapulco supplied with food by sea while other commerce was merely shifted north to another port.

After six months, Morelos abandoned the siege and headed inland along the China Road to the town of Chilpancingo, where he set about drilling and training his men. In late summer the news of Hidalgo's execution came as a demoralizing blow, but Morelos was determined to continue the fight. Profiting by Hidalgo's mistakes, he resolved never again to send a rabble army against well-seasoned troops. He sent an invitation to other revolutionary and guerrilla units to join him and returned to the job of training his volunteers. During the remaining months of 1811, while General Calleja's soldiers moved systematically from one city to another in the north, many men who had served under Hidalgo answered Morelos' summons and fled south to Chilpancingo.

Soon there were others in the army with more military experience, but Morelos, who already displayed skill for organization, remained leader. As a general he was as unprepossessing in appearance as he had been as a student. His military jacket was too large, often dirty, and looked as though he slept in it. Instead of a hat, he wore a white bandana tied about his head. But he was tough, energetic, and self-sacrificing, and he won the devotion of his men.

By February, 1812, Morelos was ready to make his first

stand against Calleja, choosing the city of Cuautla, located halfway between Mexico City and Chilpancingo. Bounded by a wall on one side, a river on the other, and with two thick-walled monasteries at either end, the city offered an ideal situation for defense.

Shortly after Morelos entered Cuautla with 4,000 soldiers, the Spanish forces opened their attack. When his soldiers failed to storm the walls of the city, General Calleja brought up his heavy siege guns. After the first twenty-four hours of shelling, the townspeople overcame their terror. The children even made a game of hunting Spanish cannonballs in the rubble and bringing them to Morelos' men to be used for their own guns. After four days, Calleja abandoned the shelling and attempted to divert the river that supplied the town with water. When this also failed, he settled down with his 8,000 troops to starve the defenders into submission.

Morelos had anticipated this possibility, but he was counting on the approaching rainy season with its assorted ills and fevers to drive Calleja off the plains. Weeks, then months, passed and the rains failed to come. Inside Cuautla the people began to die of hunger. The survivors were reduced to eating dogs and cats, finally rats, lizards, and even the bark of the trees. When three months had passed with still no sign of rain, Morelos realized they had to break out or die.

He refused to abandon the courageous townspeople to Calleja's mercy. On the night of May 1, every living man, woman, and child was assembled at the north gates. A patrol of soldiers, their faces blackened with charcoal, slipped out and overpowered the Spanish outpost guards. Then, moving in single file with mothers muffling the mouths of the babies and younger children, they began to creep out of the city. All had escaped the walls and were well out on the plains before the alarm was sounded in the Spanish camp.

Calleja immediately ordered his cavalry in pursuit. Giving the order to scatter for the hills, Morelos and his men fought for an hour to cover the retreat before they, too, were forced to flee. When the sun came up, 3,000 bodies littered the plains, the majority of them the women, children, and townspeople who had been unable to outrun the Spaniards' horses. Morelos and most of his soldiers had managed to escape.

Calleja claimed Cuautla as a great victory, but he was booed in the streets of Mexico City. "With five Morelos, I could conquer the world," Napoleon cried when the story of the siege reached Europe. Morelos was more realistic. Retreating to Chilpancingo, he again began to drill his men for the next encounter.

For months Morelos allowed his men to rest, train, and make new preparations, but by the summer of 1812 he was ready to take the offensive again. This time his seasoned veterans, spurred on by the memory of the innocents slaughtered at Cuautla, seemed invincible. City after city fell before Morelos' forces. Cuautla was recaptured, Orizaba, Oaxaca, Acapulco were seized by the revolutionary army. By the summer of 1813, almost all of southern Mexico had been taken.

In September, Morelos summoned delegates from all of the conquered cities to meet at Chilpancingo to form his own republican government. Unlike Hidalgo, who had advocated a government loyal to the deposed Ferdinand VII, Morelos called for complete independence and the formation of a Mexican republic. Moreover, as a mestizo, he demanded equality for the lower classes. His new constitution abolished slavery and called for the enormous land holdings of both the Church and Creoles to be divided, with one half to go to the government and the other half to be distributed among the landless poor. Morelos was asked by the delegates to head the new government. He modestly refused, saying he preferred to remain the "servant of the people" by leading their army. This modesty was a tragic error.

Without the control of a single strong leader, the congressional delegates were soon quarreling among themselves. Instead of electing a single president, they decided on a three-man *junta* to head the government, which diluted authority even more.

At the same time, the Spanish government in Mexico was taking exactly the opposite steps in order to consolidate its strength. The old viceroy was sent home, and Calleja was elevated to the position of viceroy as well as general of the armies. This gave him unlimited powers to call up the resources of the country. He immediately ordered a general conscription of soldiers, consisting of Creoles as well as lower classes. Once they learned of Morelos' plans to divide their lands, many of the Creoles needed no urging to join the once-hated *gapuchines*. In Mexico, unlike the other colonies of South America, the war for independence took on the shape of a class war, with the rich pitted against the poor.

Morelos hoped to make his birthplace, Valladolid, the capital of his new republic, and in November he marched north at the head of 6,000 soldiers to seize the city. Valladolid was located on a high plateau, with occasional small hills rising from the otherwise flat plain. As Morelos' soldiers were storming the city gates, three thousand crack Spanish reinforcements arrived to break up the initial attack and fight their way into the city.

Calling off the battle for that day, Morelos ordered his men to make camp on one of the nearby hills. From the outskirts of Valladolid, the Spaniards watched the rebels settle down for the night. A Creole officer, Colonel Agustín

Iturbide, who earlier that day had led a cavalry charge that broke up the attack on the gates, asked permission to lead a small body of men in a night attack on Morelos' camp.

Morelos had posted only a minimal guard, believing the hill itself was sufficient protection. Moving stealthily in the darkness, Iturbide's men overcame the outer guard, then charged up the hill on horseback almost reaching Morelos' tent. Moments after the alarm was sounded, the camp was in wild confusion. The first men out of their beds believed the entire Spanish army was attacking, and they charged down the hill. At the bottom, to their consternation, they found only the deserted plain. They turned around and started back, but the remainder of the camp was awake. Those at the top heard soldiers rushing up the slopes, and opened fire on their own men. By the time the terrible blunder was discovered, hundreds had died at the hands of their own comrades, while Iturbide, satisfied with the havoc he had created, galloped safely back to Valladolid.

The next day, before Morelos could withdraw and reorganize his demoralized men, the Spaniards attacked in full force. The battle was a debacle. Within a half hour Morelos' entire army of 6,000 either lay dead on the battlefield or had fled for their lives. Morelos himself barely escaped capture.

The defeat at Valladolid destroyed Morelos' prestige. On the orders of the still-quarreling, indecisive congress, he was removed from top command, and most of his soldiers were reassigned to other leaders. Calleja now pressed the advantage. Throughout 1814 and 1815, he moved steadily south, recapturing town after town. Time after time the republican congress was forced to flee ahead of the advancing enemy.

Finally, in the fall of 1815, they were forced to move again, this time to the town of Tehuacán. The route to the new capital lay across country held by the Spaniards, and congress asked that Morelos give them his personal escort. With 1,000 soldiers Morelos accepted the job of moving the government. All went well until the morning of November 5, when Spanish troops were sighted approaching in the distance. In spite of the pleas of his men, Morelos insisted that his life meant little compared to those of their government leaders. Morelos sent the members of congress ahead with part of the soldiers and stayed behind with the others to cover the retreat. The maneuver gave the first party the needed time to escape, but Morelos was outnumbered. After withstanding two Spanish charges, he and his men were captured.

Placed on muleback with his arms chained behind him, Morelos was led triumphantly back to Mexico City. Along the way, crowds flocked to see him, some jeering, others weeping. In Mexico City, the two trials, first by the Church then by the government were made public spectacles. Throughout the questioning, Morelos stolidly refused to recant. Found guilty of crimes against the Church, he was ordered defrocked. Found guilty of treason by the government, he was condemned to death.

So much sympathy had been aroused for Morelos that Calleja was afraid to hold the execution in the capital. Before daylight on December 22, 1815, Morelos was whisked from his cell to a waiting carriage and was taken to a small village on the outskirts of Mexico City. Throughout the journey he spoke to no one; only his lips moved in prayer.

"Lord, thou knowest if I have done well, if ill, I implore thy infinite mercy," were his final words as he knelt blindfolded before the firing squad.

Following the execution, his body was hastily buried in an unmarked grave near the local church. Years later, it was removed and reburied beside that of Hidalgo and Mexico's other heroes in the capital.

10 ❊ The Liberator Who Became King

AGUSTÍN ITURBIDE, 1783–1824

"I leave behind me in all of the country only one man capable of separating Mexico from Spain . . . and that man is Agustín Iturbide," Spanish General Calleja remarked as he sailed for Spain, after putting down the revolutions led by Father Hidalgo and José Morelos. Since Iturbide had distinguished himself by fighting for the Spaniards, the remark was intended as reassurance, not a warning.

The execution of Morelos seemed to temporarily extinguish the revolutionary spirit in Mexico. What was left of his republican government soon disintegrated, and only a few guerrilla leaders remained in the mountains of southern Mexico. Meanwhile, events were moving rapidly in Europe. Napoleon had been defeated and Ferdinand VII had been restored to the Spanish throne, bringing with him promises that he would liberalize his monarchy.

Ferdinand had no desire to open a new front in Mexico, since his newly released soldiers were boarding ships by the thousands to sail to South America and face the armies of Bolívar and San Martín. As proof of his good intentions he replaced the ruthless Calleja with a more liberal viceroy, who immediately promised pardon for all who had fought in the Mexican revolution. Exhausted by six years of warfare, thousands of Mexicans on both sides were content to lay down their arms. Agustín Iturbide was one of the few who was not completely satisfied. Having risked his life and depleted his personal fortune in support of the crown, he expected to be rewarded.

chine who had immigrated to
led near the city of Valladolid,
ne of Iturbide's birth, on Sep-
ned extensive ranch properties
inside the city itself. Iturbide's
and extremely devout. Because
of an Augustinian monk had
irth, she named her first son
stic order. All his life, Iturbide
yal to the Church.

to a seminary patronized by
sons of the wealthy, where he proved to be a wayward,
fractious student with little interest in books. By the time he
was fifteen, he had abandoned school to become an officer
in the local militia and to help supervise his father's ranch
properties. From the beginning, Iturbide liked military life,
with its drills, parades, and fancy uniforms. He was a handsome young man, almost 6 feet tall, with a stocky, muscular
build, a square face, and auburn hair and whiskers, which, his
contemporaries said, made him look more Anglo-Saxon than
Latin. When he was twenty-two, he married a local heiress
whose large dowry was added to his own already considerable
wealth.

The Iturbides were among those who supported the
gapuchine seizure of the government when Napoleon invaded
Spain. In the fall of 1810, when news of Father Hidalgo's rebellion against the Spaniards reached Valladolid, Iturbide
and his wife were at their large hacienda in the country.
Though Iturbide was recovering from a bout of fever, he
called for his horse and rode to Mexico City to offer the
government his services fighting the rebels.

During the years he had been at San Nicolás College,
Father Hidalgo had become acquainted with the Iturbide

family. He sent a message to Iturbide, offering him a commission as a lieutenant-general in his army. Iturbide turned it down. "I was satisfied that the plans of the curate were ill contrived, and that they would produce only disorder, massacre, and devastation without accomplishing the object which he had in view. . . ." he wrote of the incident later.

In Mexico City, Iturbide distinguished himself for bravery, fighting against Hidalgo's army at the mountain pass into the Valley of Mexico. It was only the first of the many times that he attracted attention for his daring during the next four years, as he fought with the Spaniards against Hidalgo's rebels, then against Morelos' southern army. With the same audacity he had displayed in his midnight attack against Morelos' camp, Iturbide, time after time, was able to take insurgent leaders and capture well-fortified outposts, where other Spanish officers had failed. He had advanced from a lieutenant at the outbreak of the rebellion to a colonel at the time of Morelos' capture.

Arrogant and self-confident, Iturbide did not hide his accomplishments. In addition to his battlefield prowess, he had contributed much to the war in the form of food, supplies, and horses. Once Ferdinand was restored to the throne, Iturbide sent several long petitions to the king, listing his exploits in detail and suggesting he be rewarded with a knighthood. When the requests went unanswered, he sought permission to go to Spain and present still another petition in person. This request was also denied, but Iturbide's pride was appeased when he was placed in command of the district around Valladolid.

Before long, Iturbide had overstepped his authority and was accused of brutality and profiteering. The complaints were ignored at first because of his family's high position, his brilliant military record, and his monetary contributions to the war. Finally there were so many complaints that he had to be called to the capital to answer the charges. Even then, the military court was reluctant to make a decision against him. As a result, Iturbide was neither judged guilty and punished, nor was he exonerated and returned to his regiment at Valladolid.

Being an officer without a command was intolerable for Iturbide. He remained in the capital, brooding, gambling, and composing endless petitions to the government, asking payment of the debt owed him. When he and his wife bought a large home on the outskirts of the capital, they had to go to money lenders for the first time in their lives. During the next four years, most of which were spent in idleness, Iturbide's resentment and dissatisfaction steadily grew.

Iturbide was not the only one who was becoming disenchanted with the new regime of Ferdinand VII. By 1820, a new current of revolution was stirring all over Mexico. Once restored to the throne, Ferdinand had soon gone back on his liberal promises, dismissed congress, and returned to an absolute monarchy. In 1820, a revolt started among the Spanish troops awaiting shipment to South America, and then spread throughout Spain. In order to remain on the throne, Ferdinand had to restore the *cortes* and form a government more liberal than any Spain had ever known before. These changes came too late to please either upper or lower classes in Mexico. To Morelos' followers the reforms were not enough; to the Creoles they were too much. If the land reforms being instituted in Spain spread to the colonies, the great holdings of the Creoles might be threatened. The Catholic Church, which was enormously rich and powerful in Mexico, also opposed this new Spanish liberalism. In Iturbide, a devout Catholic, Church leaders saw a potential champion.

Since Morelos' death, one of his lieutenants, Vicente Guerrero, had been hiding out in the mountains south of the capital. His guerrilla fighters continually attacked the rich mule trains traveling the China Road between Acapulco and the capital. To the embarrassment of the Spanish government, every campaign against them had failed. Finally, some of the Church leaders convinced the viceroy that only Agustín Iturbide possessed the ability to track Guerrero down. Before accepting the assignment, Iturbide requested that his former regiment be restored to him as his personal command. On December 20, 1820, at the head of this loyal band of cavalrymen, he headed south for the town of Teloloapan where another 1,800 troops also waited for his orders.

Iturbide did not launch an immediate campaign against Guerrero at Teloloapan as everyone had expected. Instead, he spent his time feverishly writing letters to other Creoles and Catholic leaders all over Mexico. In January, when Iturbide was asked to furnish protection for a shipment of a half million pesos moving along the China Road, he escorted the funds to Teloloapan, then wrote the viceroy that bandits along the road made it impossible to take the money farther.

A month later, on February 24, at the nearby town of Iguala his long-brewing plot finally came into the open when Iturbide announced a lengthy and detailed plan calling for Mexican independence and outlining the format for a new government. The backbone of this "Plan of Iguala" consisted of three guarantees calculated to appeal to all Mexicans, regardless of class. First, Mexico was to be independent. Second, Catholicism was to be the state religion. Third, all races and social classes were to be united. Unlike Morelos' plan for a republic, the Plan of Iguala proposed that Mexico become a constitutional monarchy with some prince of royal European blood invited to become king.

AGUSTÍN ITURBIDE

A few days later, with a great display of pomp and ceremony, Iturbide took formal command of the new "trigar-
tine" army, named for the three guarantees: "Independence,
Religion and Union."

The groundwork for the rebellion had already been laid
through Iturbide's correspondence, and by midsummer the
movement had become a juggernaught. Vicente Guerrero
came down from the mountains with his guerrillas to offer
his support. While he directed operations in the south, Iturbide led the rest of the army north. Cities that did not fall
before Iturbide's troops began to stage their own revolutions
under local leaders, declaring support of the plan. The movement gained such momentum that the smaller Captain-Generalcy of Guatemala, which included most of the countries
of Central America, also declared in favor of the plan. No
longer the ruthless conqueror, Iturbide allowed the Spanish
gapuchines to choose between remaining as citizens of the
new monarchy or taking their wealth and returning unmolested to Spain. The same offer was made to the Spanish
soldiers, who could join Iturbide's army or lay down their
arms and be given safe escort to the port of Veracruz, where
Spanish ships would take them home.

Powerless to halt a movement that seemed to appeal to
everyone, the viceroy resigned. When the new viceroy disembarked at Veracruz in August, he found the city surrounded.
It was not even possible to get to the capital to take office. In
face of such odds, he agreed to a meeting with Iturbide at a
small town just outside of Veracruz. There, on August 24, he
signed the Treaty of Córdoba, acknowledging the independence of Mexico and agreeing to the Plan of Iguala. In all
the excitement, no one really noticed that the plan had been
altered in one small detail. It no longer insisted on a monarch
of European blood, but permitted the selection of a native

Mexican if no suitable European prince could be found.

Iturbide chose his thirty-eighth birthday, September 27, 1821, for his triumphal entry into Mexico City. The honors denied him by Spain were more than made up by those awarded him by his own countrymen. Flowers were tossed from windows to line his path. He was presented with a gold key to the city on a silver platter. Since dawn the church bells of the capital had been tolling the victory, and throughout the night exploding fireworks lit the sky.

The next day Iturbide was named president of the regency that was to set up the new government, while awaiting the arrival of a suitable monarch. By February, 1822, when the first congress convened, the fireworks of victory had burned down, revealing the ashes of bankruptcy. Taking advantage of Iturbide's amnesty, the *gapuchines* had returned to Spain, taking with them most of Mexico's money, trade, and business. The soldiers of Iturbide's army were demanding a war bonus. Their Creole leaders were asking for appointments to high offices. In Spain, Ferdinand VII had denounced the Treaty of Córdoba. As for the suggestion that a European prince become Mexico's king, there was not a single response.

It was time for a bold move. On the night of May 18, 1822, a sergeant of Iturbide's old cavalry regiment suddenly ran through the company barracks as though he had gone mad. "Long live Agustín the First!" he cried.

"Long live Agustín the First!" Others of the barracks took up the cry and poured out into the streets. Soon a great, jostling mob was stumbling toward Iturbide's townhouse. Not only was Iturbide awake, but the other members of the regency had been invited to his home that evening. Throughout the night, Iturbide answered the summons of the crowd and stepped out onto a balcony briefly to let them see his face.

The Cathedral in Mexico City, where Iturbide was crowned emperor of Mexico

Early the next morning he was summoned to an emergency session of congress. "Long live Agustín the First!" the excited crowds screamed as they pulled his carriage by hand through the streets.

Not all the members of congress were in favor of the move, but by a majority of four to one Iturbide was elected king of Mexico. Outside, the crowds went wild once again.

Coronation ceremonies were held on July 21. A French dressmaker was hired to design lavish dresses for Iturbide's wife and other ladies of the court; but in imitation of Napoleon, Iturbide chose the simple, unadorned uniform of cavalry officer. The elaborate ceremonies lasted five hours. That night the sky was lit with another display of fireworks, while medals bearing the likeness of the new emperor were thrown to the throngs in the streets.

The new monarch had assumed control over a huge empire, the third largest in the world, surpassed only by China and Russia. Mexico reached from the Panamanian border in the south, including Guatemala and other Central American countries, to some undefined border in Colorado and Utah.

Sensitive to his new importance, Iturbide set up all the trappings of a royal court, from liveried lackeys to ladies- and gentlemen-in-waiting. His children and relatives were given the titles of princes and princesses. As though in memory of the knighthood refused him by Spain, he created the Order of Guadalupe, the first medals going to the members of his own family, then to officers who had shown him the most loyalty.

The Mexican people were temporarily fascinated by the pageantry and splendor of their new monarchy, but it did not take long for reality to tarnish the glamor. The country was already bankrupt. The cost of maintaining the royal court exceeded treasury funds. When the legislature failed to find a way to raise money, Iturbide summarily dismissed congress and appointed a small *junta* with dictatorial powers to serve in its place. As the money shortage became even more acute, he forced the very same landowners who had once supported him to lend the government the money. Much of the new empire's financial distress resulted from the fact that the Spanish army, though driven from the mainland, continued to hold San Juan Ulloa, an island commanding the entrance to the port of Veracruz, where they collected customs duties on incoming vessels, robbing Mexico of needed income.

Late in the year, Iturbide angrily dismissed the port commander, Antonio Santa Anna, for failing to drive out the Spaniards. The move was ill-timed. Santa Anna, who one day would become one of Mexico's great leaders, did not take the affront in good grace. Already much feeling was stirring against the emperor and on December 2, 1822, the disgruntled Santa Anna took the lead by issuing a proclamation calling for the end of the monarchy and Mexico's reorganization as a republic.

The new movement swept from town to town. Hoping to stave off disaster, Iturbide reconvened congress, but his move came too late. It was no more possible to stop this new revolutionary movement than it had been to stop his own army two years before. On March 19, 1823, Iturbide sent a letter of abdication to congress and, with the members of his family, headed by carriage for Veracruz, where all boarded an English ship that carried them to exile in Europe.

After a brief stopover in Italy, Iturbide moved to England. He then became convinced, because of rumors from other exiled Latin Americans, that Spain was secretly plotting an invasion of Mexico. He wrote to the Mexican congress, offering to return and lead their army again. The Mexican congress responded with a warning that if Iturbide ever set foot in Mexico again, he was to be executed. Unfortunately, Iturbide had already set sail by the time the answer reached England. In July, his ship hove to off the coast north of Veracruz, and Iturbide went ashore to meet friends. Recognized by local soldiers, he was seized. On July 19, 1824, Iturbide faced a firing squad at the small town of Padilla. News of his death brought protests from the conservatives in Mexico City, but it did not halt the completion of the constitution of the Republic of Mexico three months later.

If he had not set himself up as king, Iturbide might stand today beside Hidalgo and Morelos in the affection of the Mexican people. He is admired for his military achievements, but not revered. Yet, without his ruthlessness, arrogance, and daring Mexico might not have achieved her independence.

11 ❖ Indian Patriot

BENITO JUÁREZ, 1806–1872

Benito Juárez was born on March 21, 1806, in a tiny Indian village high in the mountains above the city of Oaxaca in southern Mexico. His parents, who were pure-blooded Zapotec Indians, died when he was very young and he was reared first by his grandparents, later by an uncle. There was no school in the remote village, but occasionally some of the younger people left their homes for Oaxaca, where they found work as servants, learned Spanish, and if they were very fortunate even received a little education. As he herded sheep on the rocky hillside, Juárez dreamed of going to Oaxaca, too; but his uncle, who had all he could do to provide for his own family as well as an orphaned nephew, considered education a waste of time.

In his eagerness to learn more about the outside world, Juárez talked to every traveler who stopped on his way down the mountain. One day, when he was twelve years old, while he was busy talking to a passing muleteer, someone stole one of his sheep. When Juárez discovered the loss, he was desolate. Rather than face the thrashing he knew he would receive from his uncle, he decided to run away. He left his flock in the care of another shepherd and started down the road, barefoot, penniless, and with only the clothing on his back.

In Oaxaca he asked the way to the residence of Don Antonio Mazza, where one of his older sisters was employed as a cook. The Mazzas were wealthy Italian *gapuchines*, but highly respected. They gave the twelve-year-old boy temporary shelter until they found him employment as an apprentice bookbinder for a Franciscan priest, Antonio Salanueva. As the boy was intelligent and eager to learn, Father Salanueva arranged for Juárez to attend school during the day and do his bindery work at night. Within a short time Juárez had learned Spanish. Dismayed at the segregated schools, which provided only minimal instruction for Indians, Juárez tried to make up for the loss by borrowing every book available to him. Years later, his Oaxaca neighbors remembered him mainly as a dark-skinned, sober-faced youth, habitually walking along the streets with a stack of books in his arms.

When he was fifteen, Juárez enrolled in the seminary at Oaxaca, urged by Father Salanueva to study for the priesthood. He was an excellent student, but he had no real desire to become a priest. Once his studies were completed, he found excuses to delay taking the final steps that would lead to his ordination.

By this time the revolutions led by Hidalgo, Morelos, and Iturbide had brought about Mexico's separation from Spain. In 1824 Mexico completed its new constitution, and one of the first moves of the new government was to start a school system independent of the Catholic Church. When a civil college, the Institute of Arts and Sciences, was founded at Oaxaca, Juárez left the seminary to enroll as a law student.

Establishment of the Republic of Mexico had not solved Mexico's political or internal problems. The government quickly split along class lines, with the liberal party, made up largely of the newly educated class of mestizos, opposing the conservative party, which represented the landowners and the clergy. Almost as quickly as one president took office, his government would be overthrown and the opposing party would seize control.

In 1828, Antonio Santa Anna, who had initiated the revolt

against Iturbide, was serving his first term as president. On a visit to Oaxaca, he was guest of honor at a banquet at the Institute. The top pupils had been selected to wait on the president's table, where they were introduced to him. Santa Anna's eyes traveled no farther than Juárez's bare feet. He then dismissed the boy as a person who would never become important. Years later all that Santa Anna could recall of that first meeting was that Juárez had been barefoot.

Perhaps Santa Anna would have reached the same conclusion if he had looked more closely. Juárez was of medium stature, stocky, dark-skinned, with prominent cheekbones and straight, coarse, black hair, which he wore combed across his forehead. His expression was usually rigid and unsmiling.

Juárez continued to excel in his studies and was soon acting as an assistant instructor. In 1831, when he received his law degree, he decided to go into politics, running successfully for the position of city councilman. During the next fifteen years Juárez rose steadily in importance in his native state of Oaxaca. Following his term as councilman he practiced law and served as a teacher at the Institute. Later he held the office of judge and finally was appointed secretary to the governor. His reputation for honesty, shrewdness, and hard work won him popularity with both the upper and lower classes.

Juárez's rise was not unique. The new schools had educated a whole new class of mestizo lawyers, doctors, and educators, many of whom were rising to importance in the outlying state governments. Juárez was one of the few pure-blooded Indians to join their ranks. Like Juárez, almost all were members of the liberal party.

Juárez had continued his friendship with the Mazzas and in 1843, when he was thirty-seven, he married Margarita Mazza,

BENITO JUÁREZ

daughter of the people who had first befriended him. In spite of the twenty years' difference in their ages, they were in love. The quiet, devoted Margarita, as well as her family, were able to see Juárez's true qualities.

"He is very homely, but very good," Margarita wrote to a close friend, describing her new husband.

The years had not been kind to troubled Mexico. Once the third largest nation in the world, by 1848 she had shrunk to one third of her former size. After the downfall of Emperor Iturbide, Guatemala and the countries of Central America had broken away to form their own political entities, cutting off one third of her size. Then Texas had seceded, and out of the secession had come the disastrous war with the United States, leading to the loss of another third of her territory.

During the course of the war, Juárez appeared for the first time in the federal government as a congressman from Oaxaca. Few noticed him. At a time when bombast and oratory were the rule, Juárez distinguished himself principally by his silence. Near the close of the war he was sent back to Oaxaca to fill out a term as provisional governor. Even with the defeat of the army and the capture of Mexico City, Santa Anna was determined to continue the war. He fled south to Oaxaca, hoping to raise another army there, but Juárez refused to grant him asylum and he was forced into exile.

The Oaxaca government was a debt-ridden shambles when Juárez took office. He applied himself to his new duties with such diligence that the following year he was elected to continue in the office. It was a memorable day for the forty-two-year-old Indian. It was the first time that anyone of his race had been elected to such a high office. On his inauguration day, the Indians streamed down from the mountains, bringing with them all kinds of simple gifts: ears of corn, fruit, live chickens. Aware of their poverty, Juárez's eyes filled with tears as he accepted the offerings.

Since many of the Indians had no place to sleep that night, Juárez invited them to spread their bedrolls in the corridors and patios of the lavish governor's palace. In the morning, as each Indian left he pressed a peso into his hands, telling him it was the first installment of the debt he intended to repay them.

Juárez kept his promise. Fifty new schools were constructed, many of them in Indian communities. He instituted agricultural reforms. At his direction a highway was cut through to the coast, which greatly boosted the economy. By 1852, when he left office, the government debt was all but paid off. His success had brought him to the attention of other liberals, but the political winds had changed again. Liberal leaders had failed to achieve a stable federal government, and Santa Anna had been called back from exile to head the country once more.

On leaving the governor's office, Juárez returned to his law practice. Much of his time was devoted to handling cases of his former Indian constituents. On May 27, 1853, as he was riding along a mountain road between two Indian villages, he was suddenly surrounded by a party of soldiers and placed under arrest.

The soldiers escorted him northeast on a roundabout route through the mountains. It was not until they reached the garrison at Jalapa, in the mountains above Veracruz, that Juárez realized the reason for his seizure. Jalapa was the location of the ancestral estate of Santa Anna, who had not forgotten Juárez's refusal to grant him sanctuary in Oaxaca.

After being held in the Jalapa prison for seventy-five days, Juárez was transferred to the fortress of San Juan Ulloa off the coast of Veracruz. After another twelve days of confinement, with still no formal charge brought against him, he was abruptly led from his prison and placed aboard an outbound English vessel. Juárez's clothes were in rags and he did not have one penny of his own, but compassionate passengers took up a collection to pay his fare as far as Havana. There other sympathizers collected funds to put him aboard another vessel, bound for the United States.

If Juárez felt as though he had been deserted by everyone, this changed when he stepped ashore at New Orleans. Waiting to meet him were Melchor Ocampo, the former liberal governor of the state of Michoacán, along with other political exiles who had either been forcibly expelled or had fled from Santa Anna's wrath.

The exiles faced many difficulties. None had been able to take funds out of the country, so that all had been forced to take menial jobs to support themselves. Juárez took a room in a small hotel and found a job in a cigar factory. Back in Oaxaca, Margarita opened a small general store to support the family, and from time to time she was able to send some money out of the country to help him.

The exiles worked at their humdrum jobs by day, but in the evenings they gathered at the hotel, poring over the newspapers for the latest news of Mexico. At first the future seemed bleak. Once again the conservatives wanted to make Mexico a constitutional monarchy, with a king summoned from one of the royal houses of Europe. Santa Anna was supposed to set up a temporary regency as the first step in this plan. But once restored to power, he had no intention of stepping down. His temporary appointment soon became a dictatorship.

Early in 1855, a rebellion broke out against Santa Anna at the port city of Acapulco. Leading the rebel forces were Juan Álvarez, one of the last of the officers who had fought with Morelos, and Ignacio Comonfort, a former customs collector at the port. The exiles in New Orleans did not have enough money for all to return to Mexico, so they pooled their funds to buy a single passage, choosing Juárez as the most valuable to the cause.

Juárez sailed to the Isthmus of Panama and crossed overland to the Pacific coast, where he took another vessel, arriving in Acapulco in July. He was so unprepossessing in his rumpled, threadbare clothing that an officious young officer assigned him to a routine job as a clerk. It wasn't until several days later, when letters arrived addressed to Attorney Benito Juárez that the leaders discovered his true identity. When asked why he hadn't informed everyone of his importance immediately, Juárez merely shrugged. "We all work for freedom here. What difference does it make?" he said.

Juárez was immediately assigned to help Ignacio Comonfort work out plans for a new government. The people of Mexico were tired of Santa Anna's tyranny and the new rebellion spread rapidly. Mexico City fell to the revolutionary forces, and Santa Anna fled into permanent exile. Álvarez and Comonfort rode at the head of their triumphant troops as they entered the capital, but Juárez had never pretended to be a military man. Dressed in his customary plain black suit and riding a mule described as one of the sorriest looking animals in all Mexico, he trailed, unnoticed, at the rear.

Once in the capital, however, he was appointed minister of justice and public education in Comonfort's new cabinet. Conservatives immediately opposed two laws passed by the new government. The first called for reforms in the judicial system abolishing judicial privileges of the military and clergy. The second was aimed at breaking up the large landholdings of the church. In spite of bickering, a new constitution was agreed upon in 1857, with Comonfort elected president and Juárez elected chief justice. Under the new constitution this office was the equivalent of the vice-presidency.

Comonfort, a moderate, was determined that the government would stand, even if this meant compromise. Shortly after they had taken office, he summoned Juárez to a private meeting in the National Palace, where he told him that the conservative generals were plotting to overthrow the government. Rather than sacrifice everything they had fought for, he planned to go along with them and begged Juárez to do the same. Juárez refused to compromise his principles, but he promised to keep their conversation secret.

News of the plot was already leaking out and most of the liberal members of congress fled the capital, but Juárez continued to go about his work as usual. On the morning of December 17, when he arrived for work at the National Palace, he was arrested by conservative troops, who had taken over during the night. Escorted to a small room on an upper floor of the palace, he was held under constant guard for three weeks. Early one morning he was led from the room, escorted hurriedly through back corridors to a side entrance, and released with a warning to flee. Not daring to return to his home, Juárez and his secretary, who had been freed with him, walked through the city streets as unobstrusively as possible. Even when they reached the outskirts of the capital, they could not follow the main roads for fear soldiers might overtake them. They headed north, traveling through fields, sleeping in the open, and begging food from farmers along the way.

Not until they reached Querétaro, where the remnants of congress had taken refuge, did Juárez learn why he had been released. After several weeks, Comonfort realized that it had been a mistake to believe he could compromise with the conservatives. One of his last acts before resigning the presidency and leaving the country had been to order Juárez's release.

The chief justice was the next in succession for the presidency according to the Constitution of 1857. Juárez announced from Querétaro that he was taking over the presidency. The country was stunned. For more than twenty years, when political regimes had been overthrown their leaders had gone into exile or had been executed. No one had ever called on the law before. In the capital, the conservatives were infuriated. In the country, many of the people were pleased with Juárez's stand and 7,000 men formed an army in his support.

Unfortunately, they were mostly farmers and laborers, unskilled in warfare. Even their commander, Santos Degollado, governor of Michoacán, was a college professor, not a military man. They were no match for the experienced conservative army. Juárez fled first to Guadalajara, then got in a black carriage with the other members of his congress, and went on to the coast. The black coach traveled with curtains drawn. When people asked who was inside, the coachmen replied they were members of a "sick family."

At the port of Manzanillo, Juárez and the other leaders boarded a vessel headed for Veracruz, which was still firmly held by the liberals. Once again, Juárez sailed down the west coast, crossed overland at the Isthmus, and arrived at Veracruz on the east coast in May, 1858.

The city's liberal leaders greeted Juárez and the members of congress and escorted the group to the house that would be their temporary residence. Rising early the next morning, Juárez found that there was no water in his room. He climbed to the roof of the building and found the lady of the house directing her servants as they filled basins from a large tank that held rainwater. When Juárez asked politely if he could have water also, the woman mistook him for a servant. "Get your own water. We have more important things to do this morning," she replied angrily.

Without protest, Juárez obeyed. That evening, when the same woman entered the dining room, where her guests were sitting down to a banquet, she looked at the guest of honor, screamed, and fled to the kitchen. Juárez was more amused than angered by the incident.

Years and importance had not changed his plain appearance, except that there were streaks of gray in his black hair. Unlike most of the previous presidents, he refused to wear lavish uniforms, but continued to dress in his plain, often poorly fitting, black suit.

In time, Margarita and the children joined Juárez in Veracruz, where he set up his new capital. For the next three years Mexico was torn by a civil war between the liberal government at Veracruz and the conservative government at Mexico City. Most of the nations of Europe recognized the conservatives. Only the United States recognized Juárez's government. Juárez used the customs money collected at Veracruz to support his army. To support their army, the conservatives drew on the tremendous wealth of the Catholic Church. In the desperate struggle, both sides illegally seized assets belonging to foreign investors in Mexico and many foreign-owned business establishments were destroyed in the fighting.

In the beginning, Juárez's ill-trained, ill-managed troops had little success against the superior Creole forces. The conservatives swept close enough to lay siege to Veracruz twice. Each time Juárez was saved by the onset of the yellow fever season, which drove the enemy back to the more healthful climate of the interior. Finally, out of sheer endurance and the passage of time, Juárez's rabble forces were becoming an experienced battle unit. New and more aggressive men rose to lead them. By 1859, General González Ortega, the combative young governor of Zacatecas had replaced Degollado as leader of the Juarista forces.

In 1860 the war slowly began to turn in favor of the liberals. In December of that year, Margarita persuaded Juárez to attend the local opera. During the performance a message was delivered to Juárez, saying that General Ortega had defeated the conservative army and the war was over. When Juárez announced the news to the audience, they poured into the streets in tumultuous joy.

General Ortega made one triumphant entry into Mexico City, then staged still another in the company of Degollado. By the time Juárez reached the capital, several weeks later, the people had grown bored with parades, and his black carriage slipped into the city almost unnoticed.

Once again a Mexican president faced the monumental task of hoisting a nation out of the bankruptcy left by war. Though Juárez attacked the task with vigor, nothing he did seemed to please the people. Taking advantage of their new freedom of the press, newspapers were virulent in their attacks. Despite the opposition, Juárez was popular enough to be reelected president with Ortega as chief justice.

Conservative army units still carried on guerrilla attacks outside the capital. Melchor Ocampo, Juárez's devoted friend since their exile, was captured at his country home and executed. Degollado, sent to avenge his death, was ambushed and also killed. Loss of these two staunch supporters was a great blow to Juárez. Soon Mexico faced a new and even more formidable threat. England, France, and Spain were demanding repayment for losses their citizens had suffered during the war. Unable to meet the demands, Juárez announced a two-year moratorium on all foreign debts, while he tried to stabilize the economy of the country.

Since the reign of Agustín Iturbide, conservative elements had continued to advocate a Mexican monarchy headed by a member of foreign royalty. Creole exiles abroad took their plan to Napoleon III, who now ruled France and dreamed of creating a French Empire as great as that of the uncle for whom he was named. They pointed out that by supporting a foreign prince in Mexico, France would be able to extend her influence to the Americas. The Archduke Maximilian, brother of the king of Austria, and his wife, Carlota, daughter of the king of Belgium, were approached as the most likely couple for the job.

Late in 1861 word reached Mexico City that a joint armada of warships, representing England, Spain, and France had reached Veracruz, where it intended to seize the customs and force payment of the debt. Instead of causing the collapse of Juárez's government, the news had the opposite effect. Those who had been denouncing Juárez only days before rallied to his defense. Over his protests, congress voted him dictatorial powers in order to meet the crisis.

There was little Juárez could do. The Civil War had begun in the United States, and he could expect no help from the one nation that had befriended him. He sent envoys to meet the European commanders and explain the situation. Once presented with the facts, the English and Spanish commanders understood that Mexico could not raise the money and agreed to withdraw. France persisted in her demands and added even more outrageous claims. It became evident that some plot was under way. After the British and Spanish ships had sailed,

6,000 French soldiers landed and began the march inland.

Scornful of the Mexicans' ability to defend themselves, the French launched an attack on the major city of Puebla, midway between Veracruz and the capital. The assault was repulsed with such vigor on May 5, 1862, that the date *Cinco de Mayo* has become a national holiday of Mexico. The French general withdrew to the coast with over a thousand of his men killed in a single day's fighting.

Napoleon's prestige in Europe could not stand such a defeat. By spring of 1863, 27,000 French soldiers had been landed at Veracruz to begin another march inland. This time the Mexicans, whose cannon and arms were largely war-surplus equipment purchased cheaply following the first Napoleonic wars, were powerless against the superior strength and modern arms of the invader. After a lengthy siege, the main body of the Mexican forces was starved into surrendering at Puebla, and the French army marched unopposed into Mexico City.

When they arrived on July 10, Juárez had gone, traveling north in his black carriage to set up a new seat of government at San Luis Potosí. Juárez was becoming an old hand at whipping his traveling government about the country. Forced to move still farther north to Monterrey, he delivered a message to the people, promising that he would never leave Mexican soil.

It had taken the French army so long to reach Mexico City that Maximilian and Carlota had begun to have second thoughts about accepting the throne. They insisted on a vote by the Mexican people to prove that they were really wanted. Napoleon's generals had gone too far to turn back. Soldiers were sent into the towns surrounding the capital, where only citizens known to be favorable to a monarchy were allowed to vote. In April, 1864, having been presented with what appeared to be an overwhelming summons from the people, Maximilian and Carlota set sail for Mexico. After forty years of troubled independence, Mexico had again fallen under the domination of a European nation.

The disillusionment of the new king and queen began with the cold reception they received at Veracruz, the town that had been Juárez's capital during the civil war. The climate seemed more favorable to the monarchy after they were whisked inland, where wealthy Creoles dressed in all their finery came out to greet them and curious, staring Indians lined their route. In a burst of self-confidence, Maximilian wrote to Juárez offering him a position in his new government.

He received a chilling reply that left no doubt that Juárez considered him the usurper. "It is given a man, sir, to attack the rights of others, seize their goods, assault the lives of those who defend their nationality, make their virtues crimes and one's own vice a virtue, but there is one thing beyond the reach of such perversity: the tremendous judgment of history," Juárez wrote.

By August, 1864, French troops had reached Monterrey, and Juárez was forced to flee again into the barren desert regions of the northwest. He had become the symbol of liberation to the common people. As long as he held one corner of Mexican soil they felt there was a chance of regaining their freedom. People traveled for miles just to catch a glimpse of the travel-scarred black carriage and its grim, unsmiling occupant. When they wanted to pull the carriage by hand, Juárez forbade it, insisting that this was beneath the dignity of free men.

At the town of Chihuahua, where he planned to set up his next capital, Juárez received another enthusiastic greeting. It was here that Father Hidalgo, who had launched Mexico's struggle for freedom, had been tried and executed. On the first night the people surrounded the house at which Juárez was staying and escorted him by torchlight to the courtyard of the Jesuit college where Hidalgo had been executed. Standing on the same spot where the first liberator had gone to his death, Juárez renewed his pledge never to abandon the fight.

Promises were not always easy to keep. As French troops pressed steadily north, Juárez was forced to leave Chihuahua also. He had already sent Margarita and their children to safety in the United States. General Ortega and a number of high-ranking officers had escaped from their French captors and had also reached the States. Most of the government leaders crossed the border at El Paso, Texas, but true to his promise to the Mexican people, Juárez remained on the Mexican side of the city, known today as Ciudad Juárez.

Maximilian had retained some of the reforms initiated by Juárez's government in an effort to woo the Mexican people. Consequently, many of Juárez's advisers urged him to make peace with Maximilian. Others suggested that he sell Lower California and Sonora to the United States to raise funds to continue the war. Juárez refused to listen to either suggestion. "Let the enemy conquer and rob us if such is to be our destiny; but we must never legalize a crime by delivering voluntarily what is demanded of us by force," he said.

The most serious political crisis came in the fall of 1865 as Juárez's term of office drew to an end. There was no way to call a new election. In New York, General Ortega, as chief justice, was already claiming the presidency, according to the rules of succession set down by the Constitution of 1857. The foundation of Juárez's political career had been his strict adherence to the law, but he did not trust the ambitious Ortega with Mexico's future. He announced that he was continuing in the presidency without an election, by right of the special powers given him by congress at the time of the French invasion. The decision cost him support of many of his more idealistic followers.

"Better to stand alone than in bad company," Juárez replied gruffly when friends sought to comfort him.

Added to the political crises was an even more wrenching occurence in his private life. Outwardly unemotional, Juárez had never unburdened himself even to his closest friends. Only Margarita, quiet and always in the background, had shared his doubts, fears, and hidden inner struggles. Now she wrote from Washington, D.C., that their two young sons were seriously ill. When both boys died, everything in Juárez's heart prompted him to rush to Margarita's side. But he kept his promise to their people and remained on the Mexican side of the border.

Though 1865 was a year of heartbreak and tragedy for Juárez, it also initiated events that would eventually reverse his fortune. In April, the Civil War ended in the United States. Wrestling with the problems of reconstruction, the United States was in no position to send an army to Mexico, but the government offered what support it could. Many recently discharged American soldiers volunteered to serve in the Juárista army. Stockpiles of American arms and ammunition were abandoned in remote desert areas where the Juáristas could easily slip across the border and "steal" them. The greatest aid was the diplomatic pressure that the United States applied to France.

Napoleon, like most of the rulers of Europe, had expected the Confederacy to win, and now he found himself attempting to make friends with a victorious but coldly suspicious northern government. His own people had become disenchanted with the expenditure of arms and men in Mexico. Worst of all, neighboring Prussia was threatening war, and many Frenchmen demanded that the army be brought home to protect France. Napoleon ordered a gradual withdrawal of the French troops.

In a desperate effort to secure all of Mexico before the French army withdrew, Maximilian agreed to harsh measures calling for death to all who did not support his government. The resulting slaughter of many innocent people only strengthened the determination of those who supported Juárez. As the French forces began a slow withdrawal toward Mexico City, Juárez's forces rushed to take over the vacated towns. Hundreds of men rushed to join them at each liberated town. The only uniforms of many of the soldiers were the loose-fitting white cotton pants and blouses of Mexican laborers, but the men carried American-made rifles.

The Empress Carlota returned to Europe to plead personally with Napoleon to keep his army in Mexico. Napoleon refused. Shortly thereafter, Carlota became insane and was taken by her family to Belgium, where she remained in confinement for the rest of her life. In Mexico, the French commanders urged Maximilian to abdicate and return to Europe, but leaders of the conservative party insisted that Juárez's army could be defeated. Maximilian chose to remain in Mexico, and on March 12, 1867, the last of Napoleon's troops sailed for Europe without him.

Juárez had moved his government as far south as San Luis Potosí. Maximilian, at the head of the conservative army, chose to make his stand at Querétaro, north of the capital, the same city where Hidalgo and his friends had plotted the first

The National Palace in Mexico City, where Juárez had his office

Mexican revolution. On May 15, the city fell to the Juaristas, and Maximilian was captured.

Juárez remained in San Luis Potosí, but Maximilian and his two leading generals were tried for their war crimes at Querétaro, found guilty, and sentenced to be executed. During the following weeks it seemed as though Juárez was on trial, as letters and telegrams poured in from all over the world asking that Maximilian be spared.

Juárez remained impassive to all the pleas. He had the same answer for everyone. "It is not I who takes his life, but the law and the people." Juárez knew that if Maximilian were spared, his officers would not be able to control their troops. On June 19, the former emperor and his two leading generals were executed at Querétaro. With this final act of violence, Mexico made it clear to the world that she would never be dominated by a foreign power again.

Juárez returned to the capital, where for the next five years he struggled, often fruitlessly, with problems of reconstruction. He was in his sixties now, his once sable-black hair liberally streaked with white. Again Mexico was bankrupt, and no nation in the world wanted to advance funds against her shaky economy.

Juárez pushed through reforms for schools, reduced the size and cost of the army, and effected as many economies as he could. They did not satisfy either party. When he acted forcibly he was labeled a dictator. When he failed to act he was called a weakling. Those unable to think of any other complaint said that he was growing senile. The death of Margarita in 1871 added to his burdens. In spite of opposition, he was reelected to the presidency that year, though the vote was so close that the election had to be decided by congress.

Then early on the morning of July 18, 1872, Juárez suffered a heart attack. He continued at his desk throughout most of that day, against the advice of physicians. Death came before midnight. The next day the entire nation went into mourning.

Today Juárez is revered as Mexico's greatest hero, a true son of the people, and her last and greatest liberator.

12 ⊠ Breaking the Last Chain

JOSÉ MARTÍ, 1853–1895

All of Spain's former colonies on the mainland of Central and South America had gained their independence by the end of 1824. All that remained of her once-vast New World empire were the island colonies of Cuba and Puerto Rico. Like Mexico, Cuba had a heavy concentration of Spanish residents. Not only was the island heavily garrisoned, but it was also headquarters for the Spanish fleet in the New World, making any chance for rebellion practically impossible. Long before, Cuba's native Indian population had all but died off and had been replaced by thousands of Negro slaves who worked the island's plantations and made up more than half of the population. As refugees from Haiti and Mexico poured into Cuba with their tales of the terrible carnage resulting from the revolt of the working classes, Cuba's Creole landowners were inclined to give up their ideas of independence rather than risk a similar revolution in Cuba. The wealth of their sugar and tobacco plantations continued to pour into Spain, and Cuba was called the "ever faithful isle."

Spain had learned nothing from the revolutions in the other colonies, and she continued to follow the same backward colonial policy in Cuba, sending Spaniards to fill all of that island's government offices and enforcing high tariffs that prevented trade with any nation except the mother country.

Cuba's problems were increased by repercussions of the internal unrest taking place in Spain itself. Following the loss of her mainland colonies, Spain had continued to deteriorate as a world power. During the thirty-five-year reign of Isabella II, who followed Ferdinand VII, Spain was torn with civil wars and revolts. Consequently the government of Cuba was alternately lax or fiercely dictatorial, depending upon which segment of the population was currently in control in Spain. In 1868, when Isabella was finally expelled during one of these Spanish rebellions, sympathizers in Cuba also attempted to overthrow the Queen's government in Cuba. This revolt brought about what was called the Ten Years' War. It was not a war in the true sense. The Spaniards never lost control of Cuba's cities, and the action was largely confined to guerrilla fighting in the rural districts, but unforgivable atrocities were committed on both sides.

In 1878, after Alfonso XII became King of Spain, peace was restored. Alfonso granted Cuba a more liberal government, and slavery was abolished, but the damage had been done.

Sugar had replaced tobacco as Cuba's principal crop. While tobacco could be raised profitably on small land holdings, sugar required vast acreages, so that more and more of the land of Cuba had been taken over by the wealthy upper classes. At the same time, the world had come to depend less on Cuban sugar. Other nations had learned how to extract sugar from sugar beets. Also, more-advanced methods for processing cane sugar had been discovered so that Cuba, with her backward methods, could not compete with world prices.

Typically, the Creoles passed this loss of income on to the working classes. Though the slaves were freed, most were worse off than before. They continued to live in abject poverty in their miserable little villages, tilling small, individual plots for enough to sustain their families, and working at ridiculously low wages. Their masters were no longer obliged to support them. If they starved by the thousands, this had become their own problem.

Although the United States had made several attempts to purchase Cuba from Spain, its offer had been rebuffed by both Spain and the Cubans. In the late 1880's, in an effort to bolster the Cuban economy, Spain allowed American capital to enter that island. United States investors bought many of the large plantations and installed modern machinery to produce sugar more profitably, and the island's economy improved. Americans also brought new ideas of independence and freedom to add to the unrest that had been building up. By that time the man who was to ignite the spark of independence had been born and was waiting only for an opportunity to free his homeland.

José Martí was born on January 28, 1853, in Havana, Cuba, one of the seven children of Mariano and Leonor Martí. Both his parents came from good families, his father having arrived in Cuba with a unit of the Spanish army, his mother migrating from the Canary Islands. The elder Martí was one of those men who seem to be complete misfits. After leaving the government service, he wandered from one job to another, constantly getting into minor difficulties and never earning enough to provide for his large family. Young José was quick-witted and intelligent, attracting the attention of his teachers from the first day he entered school. His father capitalized on this by taking the boy with him from time to time when he found work as an overseer on sugar plantations, using José to handle his records and bookwork. Martí was frequently taken out of school, but he always caught up with the other pupils when he returned.

Finally, when he was thirteen, he came to the attention of Rafael de Mendive, a noted Cuban poet and intellectual.

With Mendive's support, he was able to complete primary school and enter the Havana Institute of Secondary Education, where he won a number of honors and prizes in his first year. Under Mendive's tutelage, Martí began to write boyish poetry and articles on Cuba's future.

The spirit of independence was stirring in Cuba, and 1863 brought the revolt that initiated the Ten Years' War. Mendive was accused of taking part in the revolutionary movement, imprisoned, and exiled to Spain.

Martí and a young school chum named Fermín Dominguez were inspired to join the movement. They published a pamphlet called *The Limping Devils*, which lampooned Spain's censorship of the Cuban press. They also published the first and only edition of a proposed newspaper, *La Patria Libre* (*The Free Fatherland*), which was equally critical of the Spanish government. These writings, along with the fact that both boys had been students of Mendive, attracted the attention of the authorities, who temporarily did nothing because of the boys' youth.

One day Martí was visiting the Dominguez home when a squad of Spanish soldiers marched by on the street. With typical youthful recklessness the two boys leaned from an upstairs window shouting insults at the passing soldiers. A short time later, the soldiers returned and searched the house. In a desk they found a letter signed by both boys, stating that it was a dishonor to serve in the Spanish army.

This time the youths had gone too far. Both Martí and Dominguez were arrested. When they were brought to trial, each boy attempted to save the other by claiming that he was the sole author of the letter. The judge decided that Martí was the more dangerous and sentenced him to six years of hard labor at the *Presidio*, while his friend received six months in jail.

A *Presidio* prisoner was chained from waist to ankle, and an additional chain and ball were attached to his right foot. Prisoners worked all day under a broiling sun in the Havana stone quarries and were whipped if they faltered or tried to rest. Within a short time, the leg irons had cut into Martí's leg, causing scars he would carry the rest of his life. Though young and strong, he was barely seventeen and still growing. Within a few months, his health began to break under the heavy labor and meager diet.

Finally, through the efforts of his family and friends, he was removed from the *Presidio* and paroled in the care of a plantation owner on the Isle of Pines off the south coast of Cuba. On Martí's arrival at the island, his new jailer ordered the irons removed. Martí asked for a length of the chain, which he kept as a grim reminder of Spanish treatment. From an exuberant, youthful patriot, he had become a cunning and dedicated revolutionist. At first he carried the chain in his pocket, but eventually he had one link fashioned into an iron ring and wore it on a finger of his left hand. "I have suffered much, but I am convinced that I have learned to suffer. And if I had the strength for it all, and if I have the qualities to be really a man, I owe it to you alone . . . ," he wrote to his old mentor, Mendive.

Early in 1871, Martí's sentence was lightened again, and he was deported to Spain with the understanding that he could not return to Cuba until the six years of his original sentence were over. For a youth with Martí's eager mind, it was a stroke of good fortune, for the colleges of Spain were superior to any in Cuba. Immediately on his arrival, he enrolled at the University of Madrid as a law student, financing his education by tutoring the children of wealthy families and working as a translator, for he was fluent in English as well as Spanish. At the same time he contacted other Cuban intellectuals who lived in Spain and was soon winning fame as both an orator and writer.

Back in Cuba the almost continual revolts of the Ten Years' War were still in progress. One of the uprisings was among the medical students at the University of Havana, where Dominguez had enrolled after serving out his jail term. Eight of the students were executed and thirty-five others, including Domingucz, were imprisoned. If Martí had any loyalty toward Spain, this act erased it forever. His writings and speeches in favor of the Cuban students brought suggestions from the university officials that he might be well advised to leave Madrid. But the outcry raised by Martí and many others had favorable results. Dominguez was released and he went to Spain. Reunited, the boys left Madrid and enrolled at the University of Saragossa, finding lodgings with a wealthy family who favored "The Cause," as the campaign to free Cuba was being called.

In 1874, Martí graduated from the University of Saragossa. In addition to a degree in church and civil law, he had a degree in philosophy and letters, was fluent in French, English, and German; knew Hebrew, Latin, and Greek; and had studied physics, chemistry, and a number of other sciences. He had also fallen in love, but having no way to support a wife, he left Spain for Paris. Early the following year, he sailed to Mexico, where his parents were living.

Mexico had just gone through her own struggle for freedom from the French-dominated Emperor Maximilian, and Martí's liberal writings were sympathetically received. Though he was only twenty-two, he easily secured a position on the newspaper *La Revista Universal*. With his income from the newspaper and what he received for translating Victor Hugo's *Mes Fils*, he was able to support his parents. He was a slender, handsome young man with curly dark hair, brilliant, deep-set, dark eyes, a charming smile, and extremely good manners. Romantic in nature, he was attracted to a number of young women, but eventually became engaged to Carmen Zayas Bazán, daughter of a wealthy Cuban exile.

Martí was restless and unhappy. Everyone talked about "The Cause," but nothing was being done about it. In 1876, near revolution broke out in Mexico as the political strong man Porfirio Díaz wrested the presidency from the liberal vice-president who had followed Benito Juárez. Martí slipped into Cuba in disguise, suspecting that the Mexican climate might be cooling to his liberal ideas. It was a needless risk.

Those who talked freedom were no closer to achieving it than they had been when he had been exiled. Disillusioned, he left Cuba for Guatemala, where he obtained a job as a professor, teaching history, philosophy, and languages. Despite his demanding schedule as a teacher, Martí was soon busy writing pamphlets, articles, and speeches in support of Cuban freedom. In 1878, he made a hurried trip back to Mexico during Christmas to marry Carmen and take her back to Guatemala with him.

Their stay was brief. That summer, as soon as school was over, the young couple returned to Cuba. Martí's six-year sentence of exile was over, and the Ten Years' War had supposedly ended with the Zanjon Pact, in which Spain promised many reforms in the Cuban government. On his arrival in Havana, Martí went to work in the law offices of former friends who shared his political beliefs. Though he was an accredited lawyer in Spain, local restrictions kept him from serving in a higher post than that of a law clerk in Cuba, but he swallowed his pride. His son, to whom he became devoted, was born during this time and he had great hope that

JOSÉ MARTÍ

the Zanjon Pact really would bring representative government to Cuba.

Disillusionment soon set in again. Cuba had gained nothing by the pact; the Spaniards were ruling the island as arbitrarily as before. Martí returned to his revolutionary writing and speech making. On September 17, 1879, he was arrested and unceremoniously shipped to Spain again. In Spain he was unexpectedly released, just as he had been on his first deportation. With speeches and newspaper articles he tried to arouse the sympathy of the Spaniards, but discovering that his remarks were falling on deaf ears, he set sail for the United States.

In New York he found lodgings with another refugee and sent for his wife and son, who were living with her parents in Cuba. By the time his family arrived, Martí was already involved with other Cuban exiles in a plot to send General Calixto García on an expedition to free Cuba. With his fiery oratory, Martí had become the leading spokesman for the movement. However, General García's expedition was unsuccessful and the revolutionary movement temporarily broke up.

In hopes of finding new support, Martí sailed with his family to Venezuela. He was given a warm welcome and was invited to give numerous speeches at political meetings and universities. All his speeches had one theme . . . The Cause. In six months he had worn out his welcome and it was suggested as gracefully as possible that he leave the country.

Disappointed, Martí returned to New York, where he found work as a bookkeeper and added to his income with his writing. He was becoming famous as a poet, and in 1882, he published a book of verse called *Versos Libres*, but it added more to his prestige than to his income. The struggle was

becoming too much for Carmen. Completely involved in
The Cause, Martí seemed to care little about where they
lived or what hardships they had to endure. He served as
correspondent for a Buenos Aires newspaper and then briefly
as vice-consul for Uruguay, but none of the positions made
more than modest additions to his meager bookkeeper's
salary. In 1884, Carmen left him, taking their son, and returned to her family's home in Cuba. In a white-hot heat
Martí sat down and composed a poem called "God Curse
Them," which began:

> God curse them! There are mothers in the world
> Who take their children from their fathers. . . .

But somewhere along the way, Martí's complete devotion had gone to The Cause. Loss of his son and family ob-
ligations were soon forgotten as he resumed his work for
Cuba.

By this time Martí's fame was international. He was considered the spokesman for Cuban independence and was also
becoming recognized as a poet. He contributed regularly to
many literary magazines and even launched a children's magazine called Golden Age, in which he hoped to guide children into a belief in liberty and freedom. The magazine survived only a few issues.

In 1884, Generals Máximo Gómez and Antonio Maceo,
who had taken part in the Ten Years' War and since then had
been living in exile in Honduras, traveled to New York to
confer with Martí. The generals wanted a military government
in Cuba; Martí insisted on a civil government. With the
country not yet freed, they fell into such foolish bickering
over the kind of government it would have that the talks
came to nothing. "A people is not to be founded like a mili-

tary encampment," Martí observed rather loftily. But this lack of agreement delayed the move for independence for another ten years.

Martí was not idle during those years. He became the president of a group of exiles in New York, known as the Cuba Aid Society. There were other groups working for the same cause, calling themselves the Patriotic Cuban League and the Independents. While supporting himself as a journalist and writer, Martí traveled about the United States, speaking before the various groups. There were growing rumors that the United States might interest herself in Cuba's liberation, but Martí did not favor this. He wanted his people to be completely independent with no ties to any nation.

In December 1891, Martí arrived in Tampa, Florida, on one of his speaking tours. His speeches were so inspiring that he was asked to head a new party combining all the separate groups into a single Cuban Revolutionary Party. Martí believed this was the breakthrough that would allow Cuban revolutionaries to assemble their full strength. Back in New York, he lectured endlessly.

Wealthy Cubans donated money. American liberals collected funds. Cuban workers in American cigar factories pledged one day's pay a month to the revolution. Martí seemed to be everywhere at once. He flooded newspapers and magazines with letters; he traveled to Panama, Costa Rica, and Mexico to raise funds. By Christmas Day, 1894, the Cuban Revolutionary Party had three ships loaded with men, weapons, and supplies ready to leave for Cuba. A traitor in the ranks revealed the plans to the United States government, and the ships were seized before they could set sail. It was a crushing blow to Martí's hopes, but having gone this far he refused to give up.

In Cuba thousands of men had already been secretly enlisted to support the expedition. Martí could not let them wait too long. In February, 1895, he sailed from New York to Santo Domingo, where he conferred with General Gómez. The intervening years had mellowed both of them so that they knew they must stand together. Together they signed the Manifesto of Montecristi, which set forth their principles for Cuban independence and impudently declared war on Spain. Gómez was made commander-in-chief of the armies; Martí, supreme chief of the revolution. Many of the soldiers already called him *El Presidente* in honor of the office he would have once Cuba had been liberated. General Maceo planned to join them from Costa Rica.

Having reached an agreement, General Gómez begged Martí to remain behind and leave the fighting to his military men. Martí refused, insisting that his place was beside the other patriots. On April 11, Martí, along with Gómez and about a dozen men, secretly stepped ashore at the village of Playitas in Cuba. The general and some of the others knelt and kissed the ground, but Martí, who had been absent from Cuban soil for fifteen years, was too overcome to make even this dramatic gesture. Soon they were joined by other Cubans, who had been awaiting their arrival.

They learned that General Maceo had been successful in making his landing also and had already gathered 300 men. Again Gómez begged Martí to remain in safety, but with a borrowed horse and pistol Martí insisted on accompanying the troops. On May 5, they joined Maceo and two weeks later, on May 19, 1895, they had their first encounter with the Spaniards at the Battle of Dos Rios. Riding with the others in the first charge, Martí was recognized by the Spanish soldiers and killed with three bullet wounds in the chest in the opening fire.

Martí's death was a terrible blow to The Cause, but his followers continued the revolution for two years, making little headway against a powerful expeditionary force sent from Spain but winning the support of most of the people. In 1898, the United States sent the battleship *Maine* to Havana to protect American interests on the island. When the battleship was mysteriously blown up, the United States declared war on Spain. The war ended the following year, and Spain lost Cuba, Puerto Rico, and the Philippine Islands to the United States. After holding Cuba under military control for two years the United States allowed the island to form her own independent government in 1902. United States military bases were kept on the island and for many years, as Cuba was wracked with internal troubles, the frequent intervention of United States troops made her little more than a United States protectorate. It was not the glorious future Martí had planned for his homeland, but it was a beginning. Today Martí is honored as one of Cuba's greatest heroes and sometimes called her "Apostle of Freedom."

13 ⌘ After the Battle

THE RISE OF THE NEW REPUBLICS

With the Battle of Ayacucho, in 1824, the last of the mainland colonies of South America won their independence from Spain. The successful conclusion of the Latin American Revolution brought liberation. Unfortunately, it did not bring peace. For most of the new republics there was to be another fifty to one hundred years of inner turmoil and revolutions as they struggled to achieve stability in their new governments.

The immediate aftermath of the wars of independence was the great wave of nationalism that swept all of Latin America. Colonies that had been united in fighting the common enemy, Spain, now wanted to be let alone to establish their own governments. Following Bolívar's death, in 1830, Gran Colombia split up into the separate countries of Venezuela, Colombia, and Ecuador. José Páez became Venezuela's president. Backed by the strength of his *llanero* army, he dominated Venezuelan politics for the next thirty-three years. Francisco Santander returned from exile to become president of Colombia. General Juan José Flores, a former officer under Bolívar, became the president of Ecuador.

Uruguay and Paraguay, once part of Argentina and the old Viceroyalty of La Plata became separate nations. Paraguay declared its independence as early as 1814. Uruguay was briefly annexed to Brazil but became independent in 1825.

With the fall of Agustín Iturbide's monarchy in Mexico, Guatemala broke away from Mexico; and the countries that made up the former Captain-Generalcy of Guatemala formed a federation of their own, called the United Provinces of Central America. By 1841 this federation had also dissolved and Guatemala, Nicaragua, El Salvador, Honduras, and Costa Rica became independent republics. Panama remained a part of Colombia until 1903, when it too became independent.

The republics of Venezuela, Peru, Colombia, Chile, and Argentina, which had existed as separate colonies under Spanish rule, already had established borders and political identities. It was more difficult for the newly formed nations of Bolivia, Uruguay, and Paraguay, to establish national boundaries. From 1865–70 Paraguay was involved in the War of the Triple Alliance against Uruguay, Brazil and Argentina. For years Bolivia engaged in almost continual fighting with Peru along her western border. As a result of the War of the Pacific, 1879–84, with both Chile and Peru, Bolivia lost the thin corridor of land that connected her to the Pacific Ocean, thus becoming a landlocked nation. The Chaco War, against Paraguay, 1932–35, finally gave Bolivia access to the Atlantic Ocean through use of the Paraguay River; but both countries suffered severely in loss of lives and money.

Even more damaging than these wars between nations was the internal conflict in all the new republics, as rival factions fought for control of their governments. Frequent revolutions, military coups, and the disorganization of toppling political regimes slowed the economic and political growth of all the republics.

Twenty years of fighting for freedom had left most of the Latin American republics devastated and bankrupt. After three hundred years of authoritative Spanish rule, people had no experience in self-government. Illiteracy and poverty of the great mass of the population as contrasted to the wealth of the much smaller educated upper class made the problems of self-government even more difficult. José de San Martín and Bolívar had both warned that the new republics would need strong central leadership if they were to survive. In many of the countries this new leadership took the form of dictatorships.

A majority of the first presidents were military men. At the close of the Latin American revolutions most of the republics had standing armies out of all proportion to the needs of their small nations. Many of the generals were unwilling to relinquish their power. Unlike the United States, where most of the army was disbanded at the close of the American Revolution, the army was maintained in many of the Latin American countries as an instrument of political power. Whoever controlled the army was able to control the government. Gradually, as schools were established, new and more liberal leaders rose to challenge the old order. Frequently this led to more conflicts and fighting, with liberals opposing conservatives.

Even relatively peaceful Brazil did not escape this postwar turmoil. During the years when young Dom Pedro II was growing up, rival factions struggled to control the regency that ruled for the young king. After Dom Pedro assumed the monarchy in 1841, the government became more stable. He was a hard-working, unpretentious, and suprisingly liberal king and was well liked by the people. But with Brazil surrounded by republics, even the most liberal monarchy seemed outdated. A wave of republicanism swept Brazil. In 1888, when Dom Pedro signed the order making Brazil the last South American nation to free her slaves, he alienated the wealthy plantation owners who had been his strongest supporters. Before the year was over, he was dethroned by a military coup and sent into exile. After that, Brazil also went through several military dictatorships before it became the modern republic that it is today.

Following the death of Benito Juárez, Mexico came under a dictatorship also, led by Porfirio Díaz, the former leader of the Juarista army. The Díaz regime lasted thirty-five years. It brought Mexico financial prosperity but was so tyrannical that it produced the Mexican Social Revolution of 1910, with the lower classes fighting the upper classes. For a period following this revolution the government of Mexico became strongly socialist. Today it has returned to a more moderate course, but the struggle for social reform still continues.

Despite this apparent chaos, the Latin American countries slowly progressed. Constitutions were changed and rewritten. School systems were enlarged producing a new and more informed body of voters. Living standards were improved, cities modernized, light manufacturing was introduced, and new and better markets were found for Latin American exports. In most Latin American countries, agriculture is still the mainstay of the economy. Coffee, sugar, cacao, bananas, hides, and beef remain important exports. Though gold and silver are still produced, the opening of oil fields and the mining of new minerals, like copper, manganese, and nitrates have brought added prosperity to countries in which mining is a vital part of the economy.

By United States standards, the literacy rate in Latin American is still low and there still is a great disparity between the lower classes and the upper classes; but in almost all the countries the governments are trying to correct these problems.

In 1814, when Simón Bolívar wrote from Jamaica of a great canal across the Isthmus of Panama and a Federation of American States, he was called a madman. Today both dreams are a reality. In 1914 the Panama Canal was completed. In 1890 a conference of American states, held in Washington, D.C., resulted in the organization of the International Union of American Republics. From this infant organization developed the OAS, or Organization of American States, that we know today. With more than twenty member nations, the OAS works to maintain and promote the peace, security, and welfare of all Americans.

Latin America today

▩ Further Reading

Beals, Carleton, *Eagles of the Andes*. New York: Chilton, 1963.

Gray, Richard B., *José Martí, Cuban Patriot*. Gainesville: University of Florida Press, 1962.

Hamill, Hugh M., *The Hidalgo Revolt*. Gainesville: University of Florida Press, 1966.

Ives, Mabel L., *He Conquered the Andes: the Story of San Martín*. Boston: Little Brown, 1943.

Korngold, Ralph, *Citizen Toussaint*. New York: Hill and Wang, 1965.

Lansing, Marion F., *Against All Odds: Pioneers of South America*. Garden City: Doubleday, 1942.

Robertson, William S., *Iturbide of Mexico*. Durham: Duke University Press, 1952.

Robertson, William S., *Rise of the Spanish-American Republics*. New York: The Free Press, 1965.

Roeder, Ralph, *Juárez and His Mexico* (2 vols.). New York: Viking, 1947.

Stewart, Watt, and Peterson, Harold, *Builders of Latin America*. New York: Harper, 1942.

Timmons, Wilbert H., *Morelos of Mexico*. El Paso: Texas Western College Press, 1963.

Young, Bob and Jan, *Simón Bolívar*. New York: Hawthorn, 1968.

⌘ Index

Page numbers in italic indicate photographs.